A Marine

&

Her

Sensibilities

Book 4: Semper Fi in Love Series

Danette Fogarty

I would like to dedicate this book
To Friendship.
My oldest and dearest friends,
Shelley and Stacy;
And my newest and dearest friends,
Kristin, Nonie, Cathy, and Anna
And all my "girlfriends" in between
Having you in my life makes it better
than I ever could have imagined.
Thank you for believing in me
even when I didn't believe in myself.

Chapter 1:

"Hello," Emma Cantrell answered the phone in a dry tone.

Thousands of miles away in Hawaii, Abi smiled. Her friend always seemed so sarcastic. That, combined with Emma's stunning good looks, made women want to hate her but it was simply impossible to do.

Smiling, Abi answered, "Hello there, bridesmaid."

Cringing at the term, Emma tried to drum up some enthusiasm.

"So, did the Russian give you a ring or what?" she asked Abi in a dry voice.

Chuckling, Abi shook her head. "As a matter of fact," she returned, "he did yesterday. And it looks absolutely perfect."

Emma wanted to be happy for Abi, and she was on a lot of levels. But the fact remained that this was the third friend in a row to find "true love."

Knowing that Eryn, Katherine, and Abi all deserved it was beside the point. The three of them were the best friends Emma ever had and they were moving on.

Without her.

Berating herself, Emma took a breath and pasted on the smile she knew she should be wearing for her friend.

"Great," she said and asked, "so what exorbitant amount am I spending on a bridesmaid dress now?"

Abi laughed, "I don't know yet," she sighed, "I just know we're having something small in New York so our parents can be there."

'New York' Emma thought to herself, 'is a place I could have a really good time.'

Abi smiled at one of the Section Leaders as he walked past her office. She really shouldn't be calling about wedding planning while at work but it was another one of the million details she was supposed to take care of for her upcoming wedding to Gavriil Maslov.

Looking at her calendar, Abi spoke into the phone, "Okay, I'm thinking we could meet up in New York on the fifteenth of March."

"Hold on," Emma replied and pulled out her planner.

The little 5x7 inch book was her lifeline most days. If it didn't go into the planner, it just wasn't done. She scanned her calendar for March. Nothing too pressing; she'd have to rearrange some stuff but it was definitely doable.

Speaking back into the phone, Emma said, "I'm okay with it. I'm assuming we're waiting until March so these other two can pop out the kids?"

Eryn walked into Abi's office at that moment and sat down across from her friend. She mouthed, "Emma?" to Abi and smiled when Abi nodded yes.

Abi laughed, "Yes, we want them to have the babies and give them a few weeks to get back down into fighting shape."

Snarling, Eryn yelled, "Nice way to talk about your friends there, ladies!"

Emma laughed, "Tell her we didn't get her into that particular condition."

Since Abi turned her cell to speakerphone, Eryn heard Emma's sassy comment.

It was easy to see how the three of them remained friends over the years. It was light and easy every time they were together, even if it was only through a phone line.

"I'll pass on your information to Chase. I'm sure he'll be glad to know that," Eryn countered.

Emma snorted, "Like he ever doubted it," she said and smiled, "How are you doing?"

Rubbing her newly protruding belly, Eryn smiled, and answered, "Good now that I'm not throwing up all the time."

"Yeah," Emma grimaced, "I'm glad I'm not there for that."

Abi rolled her eyes. "You two, stop it. This is my phone call."

Although she was saying it sharply, both Eryn and Emma knew there was no bite to the comment.

"Okay," Emma said, "March fifteenth for dress shopping, what else?"

Looking at Eryn, Abi nodded. Eryn sighed.

Scooting forward, Eryn spoke up, "Katherine and Mitch are getting married in Virginia in two weeks." She smiled, and added, "So they can be married before she moves to Virginia."

Emma stated, "So she can have that bundle of joy there with Mitch, eh?"

Abi laughed, "Yes."

Looking back at her planner, Emma turned it ahead two weeks. That weekend, surprisingly, was not filled in so she would be open to heading to Virginia for a weekend. How come the thought of it was a little overwhelming?

"I'll be there if I'm invited," Emma said in a mocking tone.

Abi shook her head in exasperation. The woman was a fireball!

"Of course you're invited, that's why I'm calling you," Abi said, then added, "Oh yeah, and you're a bridesmaid too."

Emma replied, "Great," in a dry tone and sighed.

Eryn heard the sigh and exchanged a look with Abi. Emma sounded "off" and they would talk about it when they were all together again.

"Is that it then?" Emma asked, wanting to hang up so she could put in for leave for the dates the girls mentioned.

Taking the phone from Abi's desk, Eryn put it up to her ear and asked softly, "Is all of this okay with you?"

Knowing Eryn for so long, Emma knew where the conversation was headed and appreciated her friend's consideration. That's what made them tight as friends over the years.

Not knowing what she should say, Emma piped up, "It will have to be."

Eryn nodded and smiled before she added, "We appreciate you jumping through the hoops for us."

Smiling, Emma said, "Yeah, I'll bet."

With the teasing, it wasn't always easy to know when Emma covered up or when she was being serious. Over the years, Eryn learned that you had to give Emma space in order for her to figure it out. So that's what she would do.

They said their goodbyes and hung up.

Emma sat at her desk for a long time before jumping up and deciding that she needed to get busy if she was going to go to all of these shindigs.

An hour later, Emma was finishing up in the Admin office. She diligently filled out her leave requests and had her OIC (Officer in Charge) sign them for her. He was great about it and Emma was thankful to have a supportive boss.

Being in the Marine Corps for eighteen years, Emma learned that you had two choices. You could be professional and be labeled whatever others wanted to label you as, or you could be unprofessional and carry around a not-so-great reputation with you. She chose the former and that attitude served her well during her career in the Corps.

After she left the Admin office, she noticed she was due at a meeting for Airfield Operations in about ten minutes and, if she wasn't on time, her supportive boss may have second thoughts on approving her leave.

She made it to the meeting with a minute to spare, and sat down next to another female Marine.

Luckily, the meeting was short. It was a weekly meeting to discuss anything that was happening within the squadrons at MCAS Miramar.

As a part of Airfield Operations, Emma was in charge of the department related to Air Traffic Control. Mostly though, she made sure her boss was well informed about the goings on at the Air Station and that meant attending a lot of meetings.

The Marine Corps was still primarily male, although that fact never seemed to intimidate Emma. She viewed herself as "one of the boys," even if they didn't view her that way.

She was leaving the meeting when a friend of hers, Gunny Sheldon, came up to her.

Emma smiled and put her hand out to shake his, "Gunny, how are you?" she asked.

"Master Guns," Gunny Sheldon responded and took her hand into his, "It's been a while."

Nodding, Emma released his hand and started walking down the corridor out to the parking lot. The Gunnery Sgt. walked with her.

"It has," she answered.

Gunny Sheldon opened the door for her and said, "I wanted to say congratulations on your promotion."

"Thanks," Emma answered and nodded as she walked through the door ahead of him.

It was nice to have a man hold a door for you.

She just picked up her rank a couple of months before. It wasn't a complete surprise to her since she submitted for it and had to send in a pretty comprehensive packet about herself and her career in order to be considered for the rank. However, she was still getting used to it since she just pinned on her rank a month ago.

She remembered calling Eryn and Abi to give them the good news. Abi was just eligible to submit her package this year. She had a little less time in the Corps than Emma so it wasn't a lock to get the rank. Emma was sure that she'd be selected either this time or the next time around.

"So, what have you been up to, Gunny?" Emma asked as they neared the parking area.

Gunny Sheldon shrugged, "Same old, same old," he answered.

Emma nodded. He worked for a squadron so they were pretty set in their daily activities. That's why she was glad she was in airfield operations. It was something different almost every day.

"Listen," Gunny Sheldon said as they stopped a few feet from Emma's car, "I was wondering if you wanted to go to a party with me next week for one of the Master Sgts. on my softball team."

Emma sighed. She was asked out a lot. Even saying it in her head made her feel ugly. She was born a pretty girl and had been one ever since. Unfortunately, what some people think of as a blessing, Emma started to refer to as a curse.

She looked over at Gunnery Sgt. Dave Sheldon and smiled, "Sure," she said and nodded to him.

Walking over to her car, she shouted out, "Call me with the time and I'll be ready."

Emma got into her car and waved to the Gunny Sgt. before pulling out.

The only reason she said yes to him was because he was a friend, not some guy who wanted a pretty woman on his arm for some function. Lord knew, she'd had enough of that and just didn't want to play the games anymore.

Once she was back at her office, which was located in the Airfield Ops building and right next to the Air Traffic Control Tower, she updated her OIC with the notable points of the meeting.

The rest of the day flew by with returning phone calls and putting out some "fires" with her staff.

When the time came to go home, Emma was more than happy to cut out.

Her commute wasn't far. She managed to rent a house about fifteen minutes from the base in the nice neighborhood of Scripps Ranch.

The houses weren't estates, but they were nicely built with decent sized yards. The community was built into an area of hills so there was a lot of up and down as she made her way to the house she shared with another female Marine.

After pulling into the garage, Emma went to get the mail. Most of it was for her roommate so it went into a wicker basket near the front door.

Her roommate, Ashley, was currently out on deployment and wouldn't be back for six months. It was kind of a double edged sword being alone. You liked the privacy but the quiet could get to you.

Not that Ashley was a loud person, it was more like they each had their own interests but looked out for one another. They'd been roommates for two years now and Emma grinned as she thought that her relationship with Ashley was probably the most stable and long-lasting of any she had.

That was, of course, with the exception of Eryn and Abi.

Thinking about her friends, Emma went upstairs to change.

Both Eryn and Abi deserved to be so happy. Hell, Eryn and Chase waited over ten years to finally accept their relationship and tie the knot.

Abi was swept off her feet by a man that her parents "promised" her to. That whole thing still made Emma's head spin. It was such an outdated thought that she originally figured Abi was playing a practical joke on her. But here they were, getting married.

This business of getting married and having babies was a mystery to Emma. Her entire life consisted of pushing men away from any thoughts of "forever." She was never quite sure if it was her they wanted, or just her looks.

Figuring there was no way she was going to think her way through it, Emma decided she would go for a swim in the pool and let the rest of the world go away.

Chapter 2

The following week, Emma was sitting at her desk when her cell phone pinged.

Her morning consisted of email correspondence and helping some of the NCO's with a project. Everything at work was running smoothly so she couldn't figure out why she was so on edge.

Looking at her phone, she saw it was a text from Gunny Sheldon.

Emma, the party is tomorrow night at 7pm. I can pick you up or we can meet, it's up to you. Thanks, Dave

Smiling, Emma sent off the email she was writing and turned to pick up her phone.

Dave, we can meet wherever the party is if it's okay with you. I don't want to have you leave early if I decide to go.

After she sent the text, Emma got up to stretch her legs and get some water. When she returned to her office, there was another text from Dave.

I don't mind leaving early if you don't want to stay. It's just a congratulations party for a Master Sgt. Nothing too crazy, I'm sure. I'll pick you up at your place.

Emma sat back and sighed. If there was one thing she hated giving up, it was control. She wasn't exactly OCD about it, but she was damn close.

When she went out with someone, she always made the transportation arrangements so she'd have an easy out if things didn't go well.

She was lucky that Dave was a friend from way back so she didn't think he harbored any romantic expectations.

Without thinking too much about it, she typed her reply.

You got it, see you at 6:30 at my place.

Pushing her phone aside, Emma got back to work. Now was not the time for her to be focused on anything personal.

The next evening, Emma got home and jumped in the shower right away. She always liked to take her time getting ready for any social functions. Being rushed didn't bode well if you wanted to look good, in her opinion.

She took the time to blow dry her long hair and put it up in large rollers to curl while she applied her makeup.

Being as this was a party, she did it a little more dramatic makeup techniques, using darker colors of mauve, purple, and a silver to finish the effect.

She unrolled her hair and liked the way the curls made the softness of her hair bounce. Pulling the sides back, she tucked them up with pins to keep her hair away from her face.

Finger brushing the long tendrils gave them a messy, sexy look.

After she got dressed, she looked into the full-length mirror in her room and turned from side to side.

Her black dress was sleeveless and fell half-way down her thighs.

Adding some earrings and a dangle bracelet, Emma figured this was about as good as it got.

She walked downstairs and was getting a quick drink of water when the doorbell rang. Emma looked up to see it was 6:29pm.

"Right on time, Dave," she mumbled to herself as she went to open the front door.

Only, it wasn't Dave at the door.

Emma frowned and asked, "Can I help you?"

The man standing in front of her looked a little surprised when she opened the door so maybe he was just at the wrong place.

"Emma?" he asked.

Nodding, Emma asked him, "Yes, can I help you?"

She watched him closely, trying to determine whether he was some mass murder or rapist but she didn't get that vibe from him. He looked almost uncomfortable.

The man cleared his throat and answered, "I'm here to take you to the party. Dave, uh, said he was going to call you and let you know he was running late so he asked me to pick you up."

Emma felt kind of bad for the guy; he was all but tripping over the words. The story was a good one but she wasn't going to take some stranger's word. Instead she put up her finger.

"Hold on a second," she said and closed the door to find her phone.

After picking it up off the counter, she looked and noticed a voice mail. She pushed the listen button and Dave's voice came on.

"Em, it's Dave," he started, *"I am running late so I asked my buddy, Richards, to pick you up."*

Emma smiled at his tone. He was such a sweet guy.

"By the way," Dave added, *"Richards is a little shy so don't be too tough on him. I know you could snap him like a twig."*

Emma laughed at the last part of his message. Yep, Dave had her pegged pretty good.

After deleting the message, Emma walked back to the door and opened it up.

He stood there, looking like a kid sitting outside the principal's office. Emma smiled and cleared her throat so he knew she was there.

"Come on in," she said, "Richards, right?"

He nodded and entered the house.

Emma left the door open a little bit. Dave's call or not, she didn't know this guy.

Smiling, Emma stuck out her hand, "I'm Emma," she said.

"Braedon," he answered and took her hand.

Going with her gut, Emma figured he was a pretty straight forward guy. A kind of, "you get what you see" kind of person. His handshake was firm without squeezing.

Emma smiled, "I'll just get my purse and we can go," she said and walked into the kitchen.

They left Emma's house and walked out to his car.

Emma stopped a few feet away from the vehicle and gawked.

Parked in front of her house was a very red, and very cool looking car.

"What kind of car is this?" Emma asked.

Braedon smiled and opened up the car door for her before saying, "It's a 1969 Mustang Boss 429."

If anyone asked her, Emma wouldn't know one car from the next. But what she did know, and had learned over the years, was when to spot a car that was loved.

It was red, bright red, and the seats were done in black leather with a red stripe down the center. She slid in and felt almost giddy.

Braedon shut her door and went around to the driver's side.

He was silently cursing Sheldon for not telling him how gorgeous this Master Gunnery Sgt. Cantrell was. When she opened the door, he literally couldn't speak.

Dave's last words to him on the phone were, "Don't make a big deal over Cantrell's looks. She hates that crap."

Of course, Braedon just figured he meant that she was butch or manly or whatever the term was.

Being in the Corps, the women weren't always very feminine looking but that never bothered him as long as they did their job.

It took every ounce of restraint he had to not blab something like, "You look gorgeous," to her. She probably would have decked him.

After he got into the driver's seat, he started up the car.

Pulling away from the curb, he gunned it a little so he could show off his pride and joy.

"How long have you had this car?" Emma asked him.

She was sneaking looks of him and felt only slightly guilty about doing it.

His clothes were nice, not Hugo Boss, but pretty upscale. His hair was blond and short. He was tall and kind of skinny. Some might actually say gangly but it was hard to tell since he had on long sleeves and pants.

Braedon looked over briefly before answering. She sat there, dwarfed by his seat, and looking completely sexy.

It was like the car was made for her or something.

That thought made his body react and that wasn't going to happen so he squelched the thought.

"Uh," he answered, "since I was fifteen."

He flipped on the turn signal before continuing, "My stepdad came across it in an estate sale and thought it would be a good project car for me."

Making the turn, he relaxed so he could enjoy the drive.

"The lady who had it didn't really know what it was worth so he got it cheap and we fixed it up," he said, and shifted so he could speed up to get on the freeway.

Emma nodded. That was the most he spoke since showing up at her door and she found she liked the sound of his voice. There was a little twang in it so she was curious.

She turned to look at him, and asked "Where are you from?"

Braedon grinned, it didn't usually take people too long to detect his accent. Even after so many years away from home, it still slipped out.

"I'm from West Virginia," he answered.

Relaxing into the seat, Emma glanced out the window as the California scenery flew by them. They were heading north on the 15 Freeway and she remembered that she didn't have any idea where they were going.

Trying not to sound stupid, she asked him, "So who's this Master Sgt. they are congratulating tonight?"

Braedon looked over. Lord, she was beautiful! The sheer impact of her presence made him nervous. Given the fact that he was just this side of forty and was pretty confident in himself, being nervous was a new concept.

Remembering that she asked a question, he responded, "Me."

Now she did feel stupid.

'Great!' She thought to herself. 'He probably thinks I'm an idiot.'

"Oh," Emma said out loud, "I'm sorry."

Frowning, Braedon asked her, "Why?"

She was just digging herself in deeper. Fantastic! Trying to get some footing, she pretended to smooth out the fabric of her dress and turn partially toward him.

"Well, partly because I didn't check my cell phone to see that you were picking me up, and because I didn't know the party was for you," she said softly.

'So,' Braedon thought to himself, 'she could be ruffled.'

He looked at her and smiled, "I would want my sister to check out any guy who came to her house to pick her up," he flipped the directional on, then continued, "and since that ass, Sheldon, didn't tell you the party was for me, then how could you know?"

Emma had to laugh. His tone was dry and she got that. She was one to have a dry sense of humor too.

Now that he was talking, Emma felt a little more at ease. He made a point to give her a break and she appreciated that. Usually guys just gushed about themselves, their toys, or their moms. Braedon seemed genuinely nice.

Trying to change the subject, Emma asked, "So what are we celebrating tonight?"

He laughed, "We're celebrating the fact that I picked up Master Sgt. and didn't get killed in the process of doing it."

'Intriguing,' Emma thought.

"I know what you mean," Emma responded, "I just picked up Master Guns and it's like this long, drawn out process and you're not sure if you want to be happy or just relieved you don't have to do that again."

Braedon nodded and said, "Exactly!"

They drove along, turning off the freeway near Escondido.

Emma asked, "I didn't even ask Dave where we were going tonight. Can I ask you?"

The question was sweet and Braedon found he liked Ms. Cantrell. Master Guns or not, she was a lady.

"We're going to a country bar my brother owns," he answered and pulled into a parking lot.

Emma looked up and saw it was, indeed, a country bar. Dave probably invited her because he knew she loved country music.

Most of her friends thought she was a little nuts for it, but she didn't care. The music was friendly and relatable and sexy.

Emma glanced over and smiled, "Great," she said excitedly and meant it.

Braedon got out and walked over to her side of the car to open her door.

Out of habit, he held out his hand to help her out of the vehicle.

Without thinking, Emma took his hand. As soon as her palm touched his, she felt this shock of awareness shoot through her body. Not expecting such a reaction, she wobbled a little as she stood.

"Be careful now," Braedon said, "the parking lot isn't smooth."

Emma clung to his excuse and nodded. She would never admit that it was him that made her uneasy on her feet.

They walked up the stairs and entered the club.

Music was loudly playing and combined with the noise of the crowd inside.

Emma glanced around and smiled. She was certainly not dressed for this place in her little black dress and high heels. Oh well.

Braedon placed his hand on the small of her back to guide her toward the bar and she felt that funny zing to her system she felt outside. Damn it! Why does she have to have such a reaction to him?

They made their way through the crowd to where a group of tables were set up.

A man stood up and yelled out, "Master Sgt.!"

Others stood and joined in.

Chapter 3

Emma laughed at Braedon as he walked over to the group that was now yelling.

It was like he had his own cheering section. They were all slapping him on the back and shaking his hand. She held back and waited for him to make the rounds. It was nice to see his reception.

When she was pinned, she called her dad. After that, she called Eryn and Abi, but that was it. No party, no crazy; nothing that celebrated her success.

Braedon was accepting the congratulations by his co-workers and friends. They were a good group of Marines and he was damn lucky to be included with them.

He turned around to see Dave walk up to where Emma stood. She was watching Braedon and his friends and had an odd look on her face.

"Hey there," Dave said as he walked up behind Emma.

She turned around and smiled, "Dave," she said and hugged him quickly.

Dave hugged her back and stepped away to look at her.

"My, we look pretty dolled up tonight," he said and winked at Emma.

Rolling her eyes, "Well, you didn't tell me what kind of celebration this was or where it was so I didn't dress appropriately."

Dave shook his head, "Em, you'd look good in a paper sack at the Academy Awards," he said dryly.

She punched his arm playfully and turned back around.

When she looked up, her eyes collided with Braedon's for a second before he turned away. The weird thing was, she thought she saw a flash of anger in them for that quick second.

Dave turned around and motioned for a waitress before he guided Emma to the nearest seat.

Emma sat down and waited for Dave to join her.

Once he was seated she leaned over toward him and asked, "How do you know Master Sgt. Richards?"

The music started up and it was loud, so Dave had to practically yell for her to hear him.

"We met at a Squadron function and both play on the softball team," Dave said.

Emma nodded, remembering he mentioned that. She took a sip of the drink Dave handed to her and smiled. He remembered what drink she preferred.

Braedon sat down at the table and tried to pretend to listen to the conversations going on around him. He should be happy, they were throwing this party for him. The only thing he was really interested in was finding out how close Dave and Emma were.

One of his brother's friends came up to him and smiled. She was a cute thing, dressed in tight jeans and a t-shirt with shiny sequins on it. Her hair was teased and she had on a ton of makeup.

"Do you want to dance?" the woman asked with a knowing look.

Braedon nodded and followed her out onto the dance floor.

Emma sipped her drink and chatted with Dave. She looked around and, not seeing Braedon, scanned the room. He was out on the crowded dance floor with some woman. She was good looking, which made Emma frown.

Dave looked at Emma and asked, "Are you okay?"

Snapping out of her little pout, Emma faced him and smiled, "Yeah, why?"

This was not the friend he knew. Emma was never one to brood or look pissed. One of the things he admired most about her was the ability she had to hide her thoughts.

"You look pissed off," he answered.

Now Emma was disappointed in herself. She gave herself a mental adjustment and smiled. Her face was now devoid of emotion.

"I'm fine, just thinking about something that happened at work," she responded and hoped she wouldn't have to explain since it was nothing to do with work.

Luckily, Dave just nodded and took a drink of his beer.

Emma decided that she needed a swift kick in the ass for her thoughts over the last couple of weeks. She shouldn't be jealous of her friends or thinking about some guy she met about an hour and a half earlier. It was pitiful and not like her at all.

She excused herself and went to the restroom, needing a minute to freshen up and renew her composure.

Once she went into the stall, she stood there and took some deep breaths.

A couple of women came into the restroom after her and stood at the sinks, talking.

Emma was about to exit the stall when she heard one of them mention Braedon's name. Peering through the crack in the stall door, she saw the woman he was just dancing with standing there. She was applying makeup to a face that was already heavy with the stuff.

"He's going to go home with me tonight," the woman said, confidently.

Her friend chuckled, "Uh, I don't know about that," she handed her friend some perfume. "Did you see that woman he came in with?"

Emma cocked her head, interested to see what they would say about her.

"Oh, you mean Miss Bitch," the makeup hussy sneered, "Did you see that dress?" she asked her friend.

The friend nodded and bared her teeth to make sure there was no food stuck in them, "Yes, it's gorgeous, like she is."

Smiling, Emma was actually pleased, for once, that her looks were an asset.

The woman who hung on Braedon, shrugged, "I guess, if you like the prostitute look."

Emma leered through the door.

Running her hands down the side of her dress, she squared her shoulders and came out of the stall. Walking up to the sink, she washed her hands and took an extra amount of time drying them.

After she threw out the paper towel, she ran her fingers through her hair to give it some lift, and then turned from side to side in the mirror.

Pretending to finally notice the other two women, Emma turned to them and smiled.

"I'm pretty sure," she started in a low drawl, "that he likes the dress and everything inside it."

Without saying anything else, she strutted out of the bathroom and laughed when she was outside.

'Amateurs,' she thought.

Emma made her way back to her seat and noticed that Braedon was now sitting on the other side of Dave. As she walked up, he stood and waited behind her chair for her to sit. His actions gave her stomach a little flip and she smiled her thanks.

Braedon went back to his seat and started up his conversation with Dave.

Sitting there, Emma felt like she was being ignored. She wasn't of course, but that didn't keep her from feeling like she was. A few men smiled as they walked by but didn't stop.

Looking around for a server, she didn't see any, so she stood up and headed for the bar.

A man moved over for her, much to the disgust of his girlfriend from the looks of it. Emma nodded and smiled, but didn't comment.

"Well now." A man came over to the other side of the bar and asked her, "How can a pretty little thing like you be in my bar and I not know about it?"

Emma laughed.

Wiping down the bar, the man introduced himself. "I'm Jason, the owner of this establishment, and here at your service."

She wasn't sure if it was the drawl or the sparkle in his eyes that made her think he was adorable.

Leaning in closer, and looking a little seductive, Emma said, "Well, I've been here for about an hour so you must have very poor eyesight."

Jason leaned back and let out a hoot.

Without missing a beat, he responded, "I must have gone and lost all sense of sight to have missed such a beautiful creature such as you."

"You can make up for it by fixing me a drink," Emma said.

Nodding, Jason leaned forward, "What can I fix you, pretty lady?" he asked in a soft voice.

It didn't take Emma very long to figure out why the man owned a bar. He was engaging and had a great, outgoing personality.

"Amaretto Stone Sour," Emma answered.

She studied him as he made her drink. The only resemblance she could see between him and Braedon was their eyes. Of course, she'd only met both of them tonight so she probably shouldn't compare them.

Jason presented her drink to her with a flourish. "Are you here alone?" he asked her.

'There it is,' Emma thought, 'the you're pretty so you should go home with me innuendo.'

Emma pointed to where Braedon and Dave sat, then said, "I'm here for Braedon's party."

Jason looked over to where his brother sat, talking to some other guy. They were lost in some conversation, probably about cars, and so he'd ignore the beautiful woman. 'Some guys are just stupid,' Jason thought.

He shook his head, "Damn fools for not being right next to you, pretty lady."

Emma smiled, "I'm sure," she responded.

Jason figured she probably heard all the lines he was using a million times. Problem was, most men didn't realize there was more there than just the pretty looks.

"How about a dance?" Jason asked.

She had to admit, he was slick. Smiling, Emma didn't answer. She asked him, "How about I pay for the drink and then we'll see?"

Jason tilted his head, "How about I tell you the drink's on the house and then I come over in a few minutes and twirl you around the dance floor properly?"

Oh, Emma thought, a man who knows what buttons to push.

Without saying anything, Emma turned to go and then stopped. She turned her head around and nodded slightly before making her way back to her seat.

A few minutes later, a slow song started and Jason was beside her chair.

"I'm here to show you how it's done," he whispered into Emma's ear.

Without moving her head, Emma retorted, "We'll see about that."

He moved his hand to her elbow as she stood and they moved out to the dance floor.

Jason held her to him and started into a two-step. The song was slow so they moved in time with the music. She fit into his arms perfectly and moved with him. By the looks of her, he wouldn't have pegged her for a country music girl. By the moves of her, she definitely was.

"Well I'll be," Jason whispered into her ear as they moved.

Chuckling, Emma pulled her head back so she could see him, "Yes, surprising, isn't it?" she asked.

He shook his head, "I can't tell you the last time a woman surprised me this much," he said in a low voice.

Emma didn't answer, only moved so she was closer to him and could follow his moves.

When the song ended, he escorted her back to her chair and kissed her hand with a flourish.

"Till we meet again, ma'am," Jason said in a heavily accented tone.

Emma was pretty sure he pulled that exaggerated accent out for special occasions.

She didn't answer him, only nodded and sat back down.

Dave leaned over and asked her, "You like Jason?"

The question kind of threw her for a moment, but Emma composed herself quickly.

Looking at Dave, she used her deadly calm voice to ask, "Does it matter, Dave?"

Dave backed up, knowing he hit a nerve. That wasn't his intention. He wanted Emma to be happy. She was a good friend and he realized a long time ago he didn't have a snowball's chance in hell with her.

"Hey, I was just asking," he said defensively, then added, "Braedon looked like he was chewing on glass when he saw you two dancing."

Emma rolled her eyes. She doubted that was what happened.

Dave laughed, "I'm just observing here, Master Guns," he joked with her.

Relaxing, Emma picked up her drink.

She nodded and said, "I know, Dave, sorry."

They moved on to talk about other things. A woman came up and asked Dave to dance and he said yes but he looked scared to death as he walked out to the dance floor.

Apparently country music wasn't something he normally danced to.

Emma watched him and laughed at his sad attempt.

"Not his thing, is it?" Braedon asked from behind her.

Turning around, Emma looked at him and smiled, "I guess not," she answered.

He sat down in the seat Dave vacated.

They didn't talk, only watched Dave and the woman he was dancing with flounder around the floor.

"Did you like dancing with Jason?" Braedon asked her but he made a point of not looking at her when he asked.

The question surprised Emma but she answered him honestly, "Yes, he's a great dancer."

Nodding, Braedon added, "You're pretty good out there yourself."

"Thank you," Emma said softly.

Finally, he looked at her. "Maybe next time I'll take you dancing and you can see how I measure up."

He didn't wait for a response, only got up and walked over to where his friends were sitting down and laughing it up.

Emma sat there and stared after him before wondering, 'What the hell was that about?'

There was something about the mysterious Braedon Richards that set her on edge and intrigued her. She'd do well to leave it alone for now.

Chapter 4

The next morning, Emma woke up to her phone ringing.

Ugh! It better not be anyone for work or she'd have their heads!

"Yeah," she grumbled into the phone.

There was laughter, "Well, that's a great way to greet people who call you," Eryn said.

Rubbing the sleep out of her eyes, Emma sat up. "Well, if you wouldn't call me so early, I'd be more pleasant," she answered sarcastically.

Eryn smiled and asked, "Is that why you look so pretty with all that beauty sleep?"

The answer was, "Screw you," from Emma.

Laughing again, Eryn walked around her kitchen, getting breakfast ready. Chase was out on a morning run and she thought she'd get some wedding stuff done since she couldn't go with him.

Emma smiled and looked at her clock. Lord it was noon! 'Since when do I sleep in that late?' she wondered to herself.

"I'm just going over next weekend's events and wanted to know if you were coming alone or if you would have a plus one?" Eryn asked.

Taking a deep breath, Emma was going to say she was going alone but the thought of enduring it was too much.

Instead she cleared her throat and said, "I'm bringing someone."

The silence on the phone line was palpable.

Eryn recovered quickly enough and rattled off questions, "Who is he? What does he do? How long have you been dating?"

Emma knew her answer would provoke her friend into a long line of inquiries. Crap!

"Well, I am meeting him soon so I need to get going," she sighed, "and you'll find out all that next weekend."

Practically jumping around her kitchen, Eryn had to bite back her impulse to pump her friend for more information.

Sighing again, Emma said, "Eryn, I'm hanging up now," and waited for her friend to answer.

"Oh, okay," Eryn said.

Emma shook her head, said, "Bye," and hung up the phone.

Fifteen minutes later, Emma was dialing Dave's number. After a quick cup of coffee, she was pretty sure she could convince him to go to Mitch and Katherine's wedding with her. They'd been friends a long time so he wouldn't expect anything from her. He'd probably get a laugh out of it too.

The phone rang and he picked up on the third ring, "Hello there, Master Guns," he said brightly.

"Hello there, Dave," she answered smoothly.

Dave smiled at her tone, "What's up?" he asked.

'Here goes,' Emma said to herself and cleared her throat.

"Well," she started, "I have this wedding thing in Virginia next weekend, a baby shower thing in a month in Hawaii, and another wedding in April. Since all of my girlfriends are getting married and knocked up, I need a date."

The words were blurted out so quickly, they didn't even make sense to her. Maybe Dave wouldn't think it was any big deal.

Dave said, "Uh," and paused, "You're asking me to go with you to a wedding next weekend in Virginia?"

Emma nodded, "Yes, I am."

Dave was surprised by the invitation. He didn't consider them close enough that she would choose him to be her escort to those kinds of functions.

"I'd love to," Dave answered.

Emma mouthed a quick, silent, 'Yes.'

Looking at his calendar, Dave ran his fingers over the dates and landed on the next weekend.

He blew out a breath and said, "But I can't next weekend."

Her elation deflated like a popped balloon, "Why not?" she asked him.

"My squadron is volunteering for a Habitat for Humanity thing and I promised to be there to help," Dave answered.

Emma rolled her neck, trying to get the stress out of it. 'Great,' she thought to herself, 'who else could she ask that wouldn't think anything of it?'

Dave frowned and said, "I'm really sorry, Emma."

"I know you are, don't worry about it," she answered.

They said their goodbyes and hung up the phone.

Plopping down on her sofa, Emma wondered what she was going to do now.

Eryn was expecting her to bring a date and Emma was pretty sure she already called both Abi and Katherine and told them.

Standing up, Emma figured there was only one thing to do now….hit the bag.

A half hour later, she was in her garage and hitting the Heavy Bag Dave helped her install last year.

The thing was a Godsend as far as Emma was concerned. Any time she needed to work out any kind of aggravation or stress, she went out and beat the crap out of the bag.

She turned up her radio so it pumped out rock music and started to pummel the bag.

Braedon pulled up in front of Emma's house and sat in his car.

"What are you doing here?" he asked himself for the hundredth time since he left his place.

When he went home last night, he found her bracelet in the passenger seat of his car.

He figured he could just call her or give it to Dave next week at work, but then he thought it would be a good excuse to see her again.

He acted like an ass the night before and he needed to apologize to her. His mama would tan his hide if she saw him being that jealous of his brother.

He got out of the car and walked around it to the front door.

Almost to the front stoop, Braedon stopped when he heard loud music come from the garage. That was followed with a loud "whomp."

Curious, he turned and walked around to where there was a window on the far side of the house. He looked inside to see Emma working on a punching bag. It looked like she was chasing the devil himself, the way her face looked.

He knocked on the window to get her attention but she didn't stop hitting the piece of equipment.

There was a man door to his right so he walked over and knocked loudly. The music was turned down and there was silence. He knocked again, a little louder, and then stepped back.

Emma was working out when she saw something out of the corner of her eye by the window. That was followed by a knock at her garage door. 'Crap,' she thought to herself, 'Are the neighbors complaining about the music?'

Walking over to the door, she unlocked it and opened it slowly.

She stopped and looked surprised when she saw Braedon standing there.

"Hey, I brought you your bracelet," he said and held it up like a peace offering.

The man sure did surprise her. She noticed he looked at her like she was an alien or something.

Rubbing her hand down her face, Emma composed herself enough to say, "Hi, Braedon, why don't you come on in?" Then she stepped back so he could enter.

Once he was inside, he turned to her and said, "I'm sorry to interrupt your work out."

Emma waved her hand, "It's fine, I can beat the crap out of that bag any time I want."

Braedon gestured for her to precede him so she turned to enter the house.

As he walked through her garage, he noticed how neatly everything was. 'Impressive for a place where a woman lives,' he thought.

They walked into the kitchen and Emma went to the refrigerator to get out a water. She motioned one toward Braedon and he nodded yes.

She set down the waters on the bar and grabbed the first stool.

After she was seated, she realized that she was sitting there in only a sports bra and bike shorts. Not very lady-like.

"Excuse me," she said and stood up, "I'll be right back."

Emma ran upstairs and into her room to grab a t-shirt.

Braedon watched her go and smiled. It was refreshing to be around a woman who knew that you didn't need to show a lot of skin to get attention. At least that was his take on it.

A few minutes later, Emma came back downstairs and found Braedon in the living room. He was looking at some pictures she had up on the wall of her family.

He turned and smiled at her to acknowledge her presence.

"My crazy family," Emma said as she came over to where he stood.

Pointing at the first picture, Emma explained, "That's my dad."

Braedon nodded and smiled at the photograph. It was of a man in a Marine uniform.

Emma walked over to the sofa and sat down. "He wanted a son so bad but, ironically, he ended up with four girls instead," she said with a smile.

Braedon joined her on the sofa and handed her the water he brought with him from the kitchen.

"I'm sure he was glad to have all of you," he commented.

She nodded, and asked, "How about you? Is Jason your only sibling?"

Snorting, Braedon said, "I wish."

Emma laughed.

He began, "Jason and I were born only a year apart so we share a lot of the same interests." He took a drink of water, then continued, "My dad died when I was eight so my mom remarried."

Nodding, Emma waited for him to speak.

"He was a pretty decent guy," Braedon said, "still is. But he and mom had three more kids together and I think Jason and me kind of felt like we were just add-ons."

That was so sad to Emma's way of thinking. She reached over and placed her hand on Braedon's.

Her impromptu gesture embarrassed Braedon. He didn't need her pity.

"Anyway," he said and stood back up, "it's old news now."

If there was one thing Emma was pretty sure about, it was that when family was involved, old news was not necessarily settled.

She stood back up and walked over to another picture. "This one," she said, pointing to it, "is of my grandparents at their wedding."

He appreciated her letting him off the hook. He surely hadn't meant to reveal something so personal to her.

"So," Braedon said, trying to change the subject, "why were you beating the stuffing out of that bag out there?" He pointed toward the garage.

Emma blew out a breath, "Oh that," she said. "I was just pissed because I'm supposed to go to my friends' wedding next weekend in Virginia and I told them I was bringing a friend with me and now Dave can't go so I'm going to look like an idiot when I show up alone."

Standing there, Braedon wasn't sure if that rushed explanation made a whole lot of sense so he asked, "Excuse me?"

Plopping back down on the sofa, Emma sighed.

"I'm sorry," she said to him. "I'm just getting tired of feeling like a third wheel."

That particular feeling was one that Braedon was all too familiar with. He sat down next to her.

"If you need a date, I'll go with you," he offered.

Emma stared at him as if he was speaking a foreign language. Shock washed across her face as his words sunk in.

Braedon held up his hands, "It's not like that," he said quickly, "I know it's just to show that you aren't alone. I don't expect anything from you romantically."

On one hand, Emma was excited that he understood what she needed. On the other hand, she was fighting the feelings of being offended since he didn't seem to see her as a romantic possibility.

Since she was just sitting there and looking at him like he had two heads, Braedon assumed he probably crossed a line. After all, they only met last night. It was a little fast for him to offer to fly across the country for a wedding for people he didn't know.

He stood up and looked down at Emma, "I'm sorry," he said and started toward the front door.

"Wait," Emma said when he was opening the front door.

He turned around and looked at her; he could see the conflict in her eyes.

Emma stood up and walked over to where he stood. She wasn't sure what she was doing here, only that he offered her a life line.

"Okay," she said and smiled.

Braedon's eyebrows rose up. "Really?" he asked her.

She smiled and nodded, "Yes, as long as we agree on a few points."

He closed the front door and took her hand to lead her into the kitchen. He pulled out a stool for her to sit on at the bar and then sat down on the one next to it.

Clearing his throat, Braedon said, "Okay, shoot."

'Poor man,' she thought, 'he has no idea what he's in for.'

Grabbing a notepad, Emma found a pen nearby and started writing.

"Okay, I am paying for your airfare, no questions asked," she said directly.

Knowing he was in negotiations, Braedon leaned back and crossed his arms. After a minute of thinking, he nodded.

Emma jotted down some information and said, "And you'll have to come for dinner a few nights this week so we can work on our story."

Even though he nodded solemnly and tried to look serious, on the inside he was happy to oblige.

"I'll get on my computer to get your ticket and you'll have to ask for leave since its Thursday through Monday."

He didn't think that would be a problem since he had about forty-five days of leave on the books. There wasn't anything crazy going on at work so he was pretty sure his boss wouldn't mind.

Emma thought for a moment, then asked, "Can you come for dinner tomorrow?"

Braedon nodded yes.

She got up to walk him out. He followed her to the door and handed her the bracelet he came over to give her. He never thought he'd be grateful for a piece of jewelry but he was today.

"One last thing!" Emma yelled as he was getting into his car.

He stopped and yelled back, "What?"

She smiled and asked, "Do you like Italian?"

Smiling, Braedon nodded and got into his car.

Emma stood there and watched him drive off, thinking that this was about the weirdest day ever.

Chapter 5

The next day was Sunday so Emma got up early and went to church. She always liked going to church, although most of her friends weren't aware she attended regularly.

To Emma, religion was like sex and politics; it was private and should remain so.

When she got home, she sat down and tried to decide what to make for dinner tonight.

She asked him about Italian so she better find a great recipe to make him.

The night before she took care of his plane ticket. It was definitely more expensive but she was lucky to get him on her flight and link the reservations so they would be seated next to one another.

Mitch's parents were hosting the wedding and they lived in Delaware. There were no major airports nearby so everyone was flying into Philadelphia and then driving down to where the wedding would be held.

Normally the trip would be another adventure Emma was happy to go on but this time it would be weird. She was the only one of them who wasn't "paired up." Not that she honestly believed that she had to be in a relationship to be happy, but it would be reassuring to have Braedon there. Even if it was just for company.

Shaking off the thoughts, Emma got up and started getting out ingredients for dinner.

Two hours later, she was upstairs trying to figure out what to wear.

She was on her third outfit when her phone went off.

It was a text from Abi.

Ok, spill it. Who are you bringing and why are we just hearing about him now?

Smiling, Emma texted her reply.

His name is Braedon and you are all too busy getting married and making babies so it didn't seem important. Besides, you'll meet him in a few days. ☺

Re-reading her text, Emma thought it could be misconstrued as being rude but it was the truth. She wasn't ignored by her friends, they were just busy.

I want details, woman! We've got a bet going on what he looks like.

Emma shook her head. Leave it to them to come up with that.

She considered her reply before sending it but thought it would give Abi something to chew on.

He's tall, blond, has the most unusual looking beard that goes down about 6 inches below his chin. It covers up his horrible facial scars he got in a motorcycle accident years ago so be sure not to say anything......

After she sent it, she chuckled and went back to her closet to figure out how not to look like a desperate woman.

Braedon glanced at the passenger seat of his car for the twentieth time since he left home. There was a large bouquet of flowers there. His mother drilled into him and Jason that women liked flowers, but now he was wondering if this was over-doing it a bit.

Fifteen minutes later he was pulling up in front of Emma's house and wondering what he got himself into. This was crazy. She didn't go out with guys like him and yet she agreed, even though he was a virtual stranger, to let him escort her to a wedding next weekend.

Getting out of his car, he squared his shoulders and looked at this like any other challenge. You go in with your head high and look like you know what you're doing.

The doorbell rang and Emma walked into the living room to get it.

She opened it up and was shocked to see Braedon standing there with a huge bouquet of flowers.

"Oh!" she exclaimed, "come on in."

Braedon walked in and awkwardly handed her the bouquet before saying, "I hope you like them."

Emma nodded, "Oh yes, I love them," she said and took them from him.

They walked into the kitchen and Emma went right to the sink to get out a vase and fill it with water for the flowers.

Sitting at the bar, Braedon watched her get out a vase, fill it with some water, and carefully pull the flowers out of their plastic wrap and put them in the vase.

When she finished, the bouquet looked like it was professionally displayed.

"You do good work," he said to her.

She eyed up the bouquet and answered, "It's easy, they're gorgeous."

Braedon made a mental note to bring her flowers whenever he could if it made her look this happy.

Shaking herself out of her trance, Emma looked over and smiled at him.

"I hope you're hungry," she said and went over to peek in the oven.

Braedon nodded and responded, "Yes, ma'am."

The eagerness in his voice gave Emma a thrum of excitement. What was going on here? She didn't get like this around men.

Deciding she needed to put up her usual wall of distance, she squared her shoulders and pulled out the pan of lasagna she made.

When she turned around, Braedon was there with oven mitts and gently took the pan from her.

"Where would you like me to put this?" he asked Emma.

She didn't know how to answer, "Uh," she said.

Braedon smiled, "My momma told me that I'd better not be one of those men who just sat there and expected to be served dinner; I'd better get up and help out."

Emma couldn't help it, she giggled. The way he said it was so cute and the way the word momma was inflected, she could tell he cared a lot for his mom.

"I've got the dining room table already set," she answered and led the way.

Carrying the pan, Braedon followed her into the dining room and was impressed. She had the table set with cloth napkins and candles.

He set the pan down and pulled her chair back for her.

"Thank you," Emma said when he waited for her to sit first.

Braedon sat down and smiled. "I'm going to have to use my manners tonight," he said as he nodded to the table.

Shaking her head, Emma smiled back.

The salads were prepared already and set at their places.

"Would you mind if we said grace?" Braedon asked her.

Surprised at the question, it took Emma a moment to answer. She replied, "Of course."

They each said grace privately and then looked up at one another and smiled.

'How come this is so easy?' Emma wondered to herself.

She watched Braedon dig into his salad and started to cut the lasagna.

Once they were eating, it was quiet, except for the music Emma played quietly in the background. It was a compilation of slow country music she thought was relaxing.

Braedon ate but stole glances at Emma during the meal. He wasn't sure what to say to her.

After they were done, Emma spoke first.

"I hope you liked it," she said.

Nodding, Braedon wiped his mouth with his napkin, and answered, "Yes, ma'am. That was the best meal I've had in a good long while."

Emma beamed. "Good," she said and started to clear the dishes.

Braedon jumped up right away to help her take dishes into the kitchen and even helped her wash them.

They were wiping down the last of them when Emma asked, "How come you're not married yet?"

She felt slightly bad for asking such a personal question but she was genuinely curious. He was polite and helpful and brought flowers. Most women might take that as him being the perfect guy. Not her of course, but some women.

Looking out the window, Braedon considered the question before he answered her.

"I guess I've just never been able to find someone that got me or that I got," he said slowly.

Emma thought that was understandable, she felt the same way most of the time.

She took the dish from him and put it in the cupboard before adding, "Well, don't forget dessert. I baked a cake."

Rubbing his belly, Braedon blew out a breath and said, "I'm going to have to do some major PT after this."

Laughing, Emma replied, "I think we both will."

She took her glass of wine from the counter and walked into the living room, Braedon following her.

They sat down on the sofa and enjoyed the quiet for a few minutes before he started talking.

"I wasn't able to reach my boss to put in my leave request today so I'll do that first thing tomorrow," Braedon said.

Emma nodded, "Great, I got the tickets all set up yesterday."

He was impressed at Emma's organization.

Braedon put his wine glass down on the coffee table and leaned back so he could look at Emma. There were some things they needed to work out.

"First off," he started, "I need to thank you for dinner."

Emma shrugged, "No problem," she answered.

She knew he wanted to say more but, for some reason, he sat there and looked at her.

They were each quiet for a few minutes before Emma couldn't take it. She didn't know if it was tension or just plain impatience on her part but being quiet was getting to her.

"I guess," she said, "we should get our story straight before we get together with the rest of them."

Braedon knew she was being dry and thought it was cute.

He nodded and asked, "Okay, how did we meet?"

"Easy," Emma responded, "we met through a mutual friend."

'Plausible,' Braedon thought so he nodded in agreement.

Concentrating, he tried to figure out what other questions her friends may have for them, "Uh, how long have we been dating?" he asked.

Emma pursed her lips in thought.

She took a sip of her wine and said, "How about a month or so? That way we're still new but it doesn't seem like I dragged you to a wedding."

He chuckled and said, "I don't think the word "dragged" applies here but I get what you're saying."

Emma sat there and watched him. He was dressed casually in jeans and a nice collared shirt. His hair was a little mussed but it looked good. She cocked her head to the side and studied him.

Braedon watched Emma look at him and asked her, "What are you looking at?"

The way in which he asked the question made her feel like she got caught doing something she wasn't supposed to be doing.

"I'm just studying you," she answered, then added, "I like your shirt."

Puzzled, Braedon just said, "Okay."

Thinking that honesty was the best policy, Emma sat forward.

"I don't know what makes you tick," she said.

'Funny,' Braedon thought to himself, 'that's just what I wondered about you.'

He wouldn't voice his thoughts though. He didn't know her well enough for that kind of talk.

He considered the question carefully, then answered, "I'm like any other guy, I guess." He shifted because he was a little uncomfortable, "I love my work in the Corps, I love working on cars, and I get fidgety when a woman asks me questions like that."

Emma smiled, "I figured as much," she said then she placed her hand on the arm he had draped across the back of the sofa, and added, "but I feel like they're going to drill me about you so I need to have some facts."

Braedon felt sorry for her. Friends, although well-meaning, were nosy. He didn't have a lot of good friends, but he had a few and they could be pushy if they thought he was holding out on them.

"Why don't you tell me about them first," he suggested. "That way I feel like we've talked about them and can handle it."

'Good point,' Emma thought.

She launched into a description of her friends starting with Eryn and how they met at boot camp.

Describing Eryn was pretty easy for Emma. Her friend was a warm and giving person who fell in love with someone she worked with but had her heart broken when her father came between her and Chase.

After ten years, they were stationed together once again. Except that it was Eryn's turn to be the boss.

She watched Braedon's expression as he processed the situation. Being as he was in the Marine Corps, he could figure out all the obstacles that would present themselves in that situation.

Explaining that Chase retired so he could be with Eryn made Emma feel emotional. She wished someone would be willing to give up something for her.

After she finished with Eryn's story, she waited for Braedon to comment. He didn't.

The story of Abi was a little easier since they'd become friends through Eryn. Emma told him how Abi's parents had "promised" her to a son of their friends'.

She wanted to laugh at Braedon's expression. Hers was pretty similar.

"I know, right?" she asked when he looked at her like Abi was crazy.

Smiling, she went on to say, "But she's so happy with him." She took a sip of wine, "I still call him "the Russian" just to get her goat," she said with a look of innocence.

Braedon shook his head. He had no doubt that she would be a lady with a knack for teasing.

"Now," Emma said, "the bride and groom for next weekend..."

She went on to explain how Mitch was the one who got Chase and Eryn together. Mitch was Chase's best friend and Katherine was Eryn's cousin and how they were both on the same flight to Chase's and Eryn's wedding. They didn't tell each other that they were each in a wedding party but decided to "hook up."

It was easy to explain how surprised they were to see one another at the wedding.

She skimmed over some of the details, thinking that Braedon didn't need to know too much.

"But now they're getting married in Delaware where Mitch's parents live," she said.

Braedon sat back and considered what Emma told him.

Finally, he said, "Your friends have all had some pretty interesting situations in finding their way to one another."

Emma thought about it and nodded, "I believe you're right."

She waited for him to pick up his wine glass, then tapped hers against his in a silent toast to her friends and their journeys.

Chapter 6

Monday morning, Emma woke up feeling very rested. She smiled as she got ready for work, remembering her conversations with Braedon the day before.

She had one thing to say about him, he was a sport.

Not every guy would listen to a woman talk for hours about her friends and not run from the house screaming in frustration. But he didn't, he listened intently and asked questions about them so he was "caught up" by the time he met them.

When Emma arrived at work, she was met with a pile of paperwork to go over and a meeting with her OIC to figure out some logistical issues with some visiting aircraft squadrons.

It was lunch time before she was able to come up for air and she was famished.

Deciding she needed to get out of the office to clear her head, she went over to the food court at the Base Exchange.

She was standing in line to get some Chinese food when her phone went off.

It was a text from Braedon.

Leave approved. Good to go. What time do we leave on Friday? I forgot to ask you that yesterday. Thank you again for dinner.

Emma smiled. Such a gentleman. She typed her reply quickly.

7:15am, sorry it's early. Do you want to drive together or meet at the airport? You're welcome for dinner.

It was her turn, so she moved forward to order. Once she got her food, she sat down and noticed she had a reply from Braedon.

I don't mind picking you up.

'A man of many words,' she thought to herself.

After lunch she went back to work and managed to get a lot done during the afternoon.

Tuesday and Wednesday were much the same way for Emma. She'd go to work and do as much as possible.

It wasn't like Airfield Ops wouldn't function without her, but she liked to have everything as squared away as possible before taking leave, even if it was only for four days.

Wednesday evening she was at home when her phone rang.

Looking at it, she smiled when she saw it was Dave.

"Hello, Dave," she said in a tone mimicking the movie 2001: A Space Odyssey.

Dave snorted, "Ha ha," he said dryly, "like I never heard that one before."

Emma laughed.

"What's up?" she asked as she was going through her closet trying to decide what to pack.

Shifting in his seat, he said, "That's what I was going to ask you, Master Guns."

Confused, Emma stopped what she was doing and walked into her bedroom to sit on the bed.

She asked him, "I'm sorry?"

Dave harrumphed, "You should be. What the hell are you doing going with Master Sgt. Richards this weekend?"

If Emma didn't know better, she swore he sounded jealous. Her temper was now stirred up so she wasn't happy.

"Well, I asked you to go but you said you couldn't," she snapped into the phone, "so Braedon volunteered and I said yes."

Dave answered sharply, "I know, but you don't know him."

Okay, now she was confused.

"Let me get this straight, Dave," she said very calmly, "You ask this guy to pick me up last Friday for a party but he's not good enough to go with me to a wedding that will have about a hundred people attending?"

Sighing, Dave tried to check his voice. "I know it sounds weird but I just think you're rushing into it, you know."

Frowning, Emma asked, "Rushing into what?"

She was partly curious about what Braedon told Dave and partly pissed that Dave thought he actually had a say in her decisions.

Dave realized he sounded like an ass. Ever since he met up with Richards at lunch earlier in the day, he'd been gnawing on the information. Logically, he knew that Emma only looked at him as a friend and he shouldn't be upset about who she took to her own functions. And yet, here he was, lecturing her like some jealous boyfriend.

"I'm sorry, Emma," he said sadly, "I'm just mad that I wasn't able to go with you."

Her anger was starting to dissipate. He sounded apologetic so that helped.

Trying to clarify it for him, Emma said, "We're going as friends, Dave. That's all there is to it."

Somehow, Dave had a tough time thinking any man would only look at Emma as a "friend," but maybe she was right.

When he talked to Braedon at lunch, he related the news to Dave like it was no big deal. It was almost like he was telling his friend he was going to the doctor or something.

Even with Emma's verbal assurance and Richards' actions, Dave still felt the biting edge of jealousy.

"I'm sorry," he said tightly.

Emma smiled into the phone, "I know you are," she said.

They talked for a few more minutes then hung up after Emma promised to call him next week.

She got two more phone calls from guys asking her out and she politely declined both of them. She didn't even know how they got her number since she made a point of not giving it out but figured someone else gave it to them.

After getting most of her clothes picked out for the trip, she pulled her luggage down from the attic when her phone went off again.

"Dammit!" she yelled, and walked over to it.

The caller I.D. said Abi so Emma hit answer.

"Does he really have some sort of ZZ Top beard thing going on?" Abi asked without any preamble.

Emma laughed.

When Abi didn't answer she sighed and asked, "Does it matter if he does or not?"

There was a rustling, "Hell yes!" Abi answered.

Oh these women were going to be the death of her, Emma was sure of it. But she loved them anyway.

Emma pulled her suitcase into the bedroom and unzipped it before answering, "No he doesn't."

"Ah ha," Abi yelled, "I knew it!"

Shaking her head, Emma asked, "Will you stop pestering me so I can pack and get my ass there for our friends' wedding, please?"

Abi rolled her eyes, and asked, "Yeah, yeah, are you guys still meeting us at the airport so we can all go down to Mitch's parents' house together?"

Emma replied over-sweetly, "If you stop harassing me."

Laughing, Abi hung up without saying goodbye.

Emma put her phone down then hoisted her suitcase onto the bed and laughed while she packed. Her friends may be pain in the asses, but they were HER pain in the asses.

Thursday evening, Emma was setting her alarm for early in morning so she could be up and ready to go for their flight when Braedon called.

"Hello," Emma said and smiled.

Braedon found he liked the sound of her voice on the phone.

He responded, "Hi yourself. I'm calling to confirm appropriate attire for this weekend."

The formality in his voice made Emma want to laugh. He sounded so serious, almost desperate.

She looked at her own suitcase and said, "Well, casual for tomorrow since we're flying."

Looking in her planner, she wanted to see what they had scheduled before answering.

"It looks like a suit and tie will be just fine for the wedding," she answered, while flipping through the pages. "And on Sunday, we're going to drive around, so casual."

Braedon breathed a sigh of relief. He was afraid she'd tell him it was black tie or something like that. Not that he couldn't pull off a tux in a pinch, but he just hated not knowing.

He pulled a suit out of his closet and said, "Okay, thanks."

Emma waited for more but he was silent.

"Uh, was there anything else you wanted to discuss?" she asked him.

Shaking his head, Braedon replied, "No," but added, "Thanks for answering my question."

Floored by his lack of interest in talking to her, Emma said, "Okay then, I'll see you about 5:30am then."

He answered, "Yep," and hung up.

Emma stared at her phone for a while after he called and wondered why it bothered her so much that he wasn't calling her or texting her more.

Friday morning, Emma was up on time and ready to go when Braedon pulled up in front of her place. She was surprised that he wasn't driving his muscle car. Her question must have been on her face because he answered it as soon as he got up to her door.

"I wasn't leaving my car in the long term parking at the airport so I swapped with Jason for the weekend," Braedon said.

Danette Fogarty

His tone was so serious that Emma wanted to laugh. It seemed like the car really was his baby.

Braedon grabbed her bag and took it out to the car. He opened the trunk and put it inside next to his.

Emma locked the front door behind her. She was careful to leave a light on inside and ask her neighbor to pick up the mail for the few days she'd be gone.

He opened the car door for her and waited for her to get inside before jogging around to the other side.

After pulling away from the curb, Braedon asked, "How are you this morning?"

Smiling at him, Emma answered, "I'm usually a morning person but I'm dragging today."

Braedon nodded, "Me too."

She frowned. He looked like he was ready to run ten miles, his demeanor was so chipper.

He looked over and said, "I hide it well."

Emma nodded and thought, 'Apparently so.'

They drove the rest of the way to the airport in relative silence. Braedon turned on some music but they didn't speak.

Braedon parked in long-term parking and got out their bags. He offered to take Emma's bag but she declined.

There are some things a lady needed to handle herself.

She mentioned that she'd already checked them in online, so they only needed to print out their boarding passes and check their bags.

They were in line to check in and Braedon was standing behind her examining everything he could about her.

Her hair was down in a low ponytail today. He hadn't realized how long it actually was before now. Not that he had spent a ton of time with her, but she wore it up or curled the last couple of times they were together.

It was a beautiful light brown and looked full and soft. He wanted to touch it to test its softness but he figured she would deck him for that.

He was still thinking about her hair when he noticed that she was standing there and staring at him with a weird expression on her face.

"Are you okay?" Emma asked Braedon, "You were zoning out there."

Nodding, Braedon blushed with embarrassment, but managed to say, "I'm good."

They got their bags checked and printed the boarding passes with ease.

After a short wait for security, they were on their way to the gate.

Emma excused herself to use the restroom so Braedon found them some seats in the gate waiting area.

He gave himself a little talk about straightening his mind out and not turning this into something it wasn't. This wasn't him meeting his girlfriend's friends. He was helping Emma out and that was all.

When Emma came back to the gate area, she looked at Braedon and thought he looked serious.

"Are you okay?" she asked again, then felt silly for doing so.

He smiled and answered, "Yeah, just going over some details in my mind."

Since he seemed to want to play it off, she would follow suit.

She said, "Okay," and sat down so she could get her bag organized for the flight.

Chapter 7

The flight was divided into two parts. They flew from San Diego to Dallas/Fort Worth first.

Emma slept almost from the moment she buckled up on the plane. She must have been exhausted because she didn't remember anything until Braedon gently touched her arm to wake her during the descent into Dallas.

"I'm sorry," she said, and yawned.

Braedon smiled and told her, "You were tired," he looked around, "everybody was pretty quiet and I even dozed off for a bit."

She nodded.

They landed easily and were seated just past the first class passengers so they got off the plane fairly quickly. The layover between flights was short and the airport was huge so they had to move fast to get to their connecting gate.

Luckily, they were each adept at traveling and got there with time to spare.

"Would you like to get something to eat that we can take on the plane?" Braedon asked her when they found their connecting gate.

Emma nodded, "Probably," she answered.

There was a few places nearby so they decided to pick up some sandwiches and chips from one of them.

Braedon got the food while Emma watched their bags in the gate area.

He was only back for a couple of minutes before they called the first boarding call.

"Good timing," Emma told him as he handed her the sandwich she ordered.

Winking at her, Braedon said, "I sure try."

Stopping cold, Emma looked at him in surprise.

He saw her face and asked, "Everything alright?"

She nodded quickly and added, "Yeah."

It wouldn't be a good time to tell him that she was secretly happy that he "almost" flirted with her.

They boarded a few minutes later for their flight to Philadelphia.

This flight was full so it took a little longer to get everyone boarded.

Emma sat in the window seat and Braedon had the center seat. She was going to offer to switch places with him but he stood abruptly and helped a pretty young lady with her bags.

"Thank you," the woman gushed to Braedon, "it's so hard to find a true gentleman these days."

Emma felt like she wanted to stand up and slap the woman, but she refrained.

Braedon sat back down and, as it turned out, the woman was assigned the aisle seat next to him.

'Great,' Emma thought.

As if that wasn't bad enough, the exasperating woman decided that she was going to take up all of Braedon's attention for the flight from Dallas to Philadelphia.

Two hours later, Emma thought she was going to scream if the woman didn't shut up.

Her name was Tricia and she was a cosmetologist. She thought Braedon's hair was just gorgeous! She had a friend she was visiting in Philadelphia and just "HAD" to go there to help her through a divorce. She also kept touching Braedon's arm and practically throwing herself at him.

It was disgusting and Emma was sure he was just being friendly. That was, until the annoying bitch handed him her phone number and he safely tucked it into his back pocket.

'What?' Emma shouted internally. 'How could he possibly fall for that bottle blonde, fake nailed, padded bra skank?'

By the time they deplaned, Emma was seething.

Braedon followed his flight companion off the plane and was happy to be rid of her. She was loud and pushy and not the type of woman he went for but his momma raised him with manners so he couldn't be rude.

In the airport terminal he turned to ask Emma a question but stopped when he saw the look on her face. There was no mistaking the anger in her eyes. A blind man could feel it coming off of her in waves.

"Hey," he said softly and pulled her over to the side so they weren't in the way of other people getting off the plane. "What's wrong?"

Emma's mouth dropped open.

Finally, she spoke. "Are you kidding me?" she asked, the sarcasm dripping off each word.

He was lost. Braedon didn't know what was wrong so he only shrugged.

Her anger was now off of the infuriating Tricia and solely placed on Braedon.

"You spent that whole flight talking and flirting with that woman!" she blurted out, not quite keeping the hurt out of her tone.

Braedon rolled his lips to keep himself from laughing. She was jealous! He would've never believed it but her body language and tone gave her away.

He had to admit, she was gorgeous when she looked upset. He had to keep himself from trying to soothe her with a hug.

Clearing his throat, he tried to remain calm, and said "I was being polite to a fellow passenger, Emma."

"Don't patronize me, Braedon," Emma snapped, "I know flirting when I see it."

Even though she was cute when she was angry, his pride took a ding at the accusation. His smile faded.

Looking down for a moment, he tried to get his temper in check before saying, "I was not flirting with her, I was listening to her go on and on and praying the flight was shorter."

Feeling foolish, Emma asked, "Really?"

Without thinking, Braedon cupped her chin with his hand, "I'm on this trip with you, Emma," he started, "you are my priority."

His words created chaos inside of her chest. Her pulse raced and she smiled.

"Now," Braedon said, "no more of this jealous talk, okay?"

Emma pulled her chin from his hand and retorted, "I wasn't jealous."

She protested a little too much to his way of thinking but he figured it would do no good in pointing it out to her.

They walked downstairs toward the baggage claim area.

Emma excused herself to the bathroom and asked Braedon to go on to their baggage carousel; she would catch up with him there.

As soon as she was in the bathroom, she looked in the mirror and snarled. Her eyes were shadowed from the weird sleeping and her hair was a rat's nest of crazy.

No wonder he paid attention to that Tricia woman, he didn't have anything better to look at.

Digging in her bag, Emma found the necessary items and went to work.

Fifteen minutes later, she came out of the ladies room feeling a lot better.

Being as their flight was so early, she didn't bother with makeup and only pulled her hair back.

Now, her hair was loose with a few natural curls in it. Her makeup was now on and she felt more ready to face Braedon.

His comment about the "jealous talk" stung and she was determined to prove him wrong. What did she have to be jealous of? That Tricia woman was atrocious and no decent man would actually take her seriously.

When she came up to the baggage carousel she beamed inwardly at the approving looks she got from several men. One of them came up to her.

"Hey there, pretty thing," he said smoothly, then asked, "Can I help you get your bags?"

Emma only smiled.

Another man came up beside him and asked her, "Are you visiting here in Philadelphia?"

He was huge and muscular and had slicked back hair.

The attention they gave her helped pacify her bruised ego. 'There,' she thought, 'take that, Tricia!'

This was the type of situation she was used to, men paying her attention. She never took it too seriously and knew how to handle it.

She still didn't see Braedon but knew he'd find her sooner or later.

Her bag came around and she reached up to grab it but was bumped by the large guy.

He said, "Let me get that for you, pretty lady."

Emma smiled and said, "Thank you," before she grabbed her bag.

The first guy walked over and offered, "We're getting a cab; can we drop you off somewhere?"

Before Emma could answer, she heard a voice from behind her say, "That's okay, guys. She already has a ride."

Turning slowly, Emma looked up to see a less than thrilled looking Braedon standing there.

For some reason, she felt like she was in trouble. He looked really pissed and she couldn't understand why.

The other two guys figured out that this situation wasn't something they wanted to be a part of so they left without another word.

Braedon was fuming! He was standing by the baggage carousel when he saw Emma coming over. His breath caught when his eyes fell on her. She was gorgeous. Of course, he thought she was gorgeous this morning when he came to the door of her house. Now she was....polished.

He was going to wave to her but saw Meathead One and Two go over to talk to her so he held back.

The longer he watched them openly flirt with her, the madder he got. It didn't help that she seemed to like their he-man tactics either. When he saw one of them get her bag, he decided it was time to intervene.

When she turned around and saw him, she looked surprised for a second and he couldn't figure out why.

"I was looking for you," Emma said.

Braedon nodded toward the two retreating men, "Yeah, I could see that."

Her temper was flaring and she tried to tamp down on it before replying, "They were being kind enough to help me with my bag."

His jaw clenched, he retorted, "I could've done that just fine."

"Well," Emma started, "maybe I needed to know that someone would think I was worth talking to."

Braedon felt his anger snap into place immediately. He closed the few feet that separated them in a few steps and looked down at her.

His voice tight, he asked, "Do you think playing games is fun?"

Emma huffed and said, "Depends on the game."

Cupping her chin again, Braedon snapped, "This isn't a game, Emma."

He stood there, staring into her eyes and couldn't quite figure out why he was so mad, only that he was and he wanted to make her pay for making him feel that way. He could see she was going to say something so, as soon as her lips parted, he moved in quickly to seal his mouth with hers.

His tongue darted inside her warm mouth and sought to feel her tongue against it. Whatever word she was going to speak turned into a kind of moan into his mouth. He knew he caught her by surprise and took full advantage of it.

Emma was going to say something smart back to him but, before she could see his intentions, he kissed her.

It wasn't a normal, "I like you" kiss either. This kiss was all heat and possession. His lips were on hers quickly and his tongue swirled around hers as if it were daring her to keep up.

She was feeling off-kilter with the bombardment of sensations pulsing through her body as soon as their lips met. The kiss was like a duel of sorts. Each of them was trying to get the upper hand but neither could quite get control.

Braedon put his hands up around Emma's neck to hold her still for the kiss.

All of his attention was put into the kiss and making it feel so good. He was getting hard and was blown away by the sheer impact their kiss was having on his body.

After a minute, he gentled the kiss. Now it was time to savor, not devour. His lips sucked on her bottom one and finally, he lifted his face so that he could see her.

Emma stood there, looking very dazed and very well kissed. Her lips were swollen and there was a pounding in her ears that she couldn't seem to get to calm down. Holy crap! How could someone so unassuming kiss like that?

"Don't think," Braedon said softly, "that because I don't say it or show it, that I don't feel it."

Not saying anything else, he grabbed the handle of her bag and started moving away from her.

Emma stood there, watching him walk away. She didn't know what to make of the kiss, or the comment after it.

She only moved when she heard someone yell, "Emma!" from behind her.

Chapter 8

Abi, Eryn, and Chase were all walking toward the baggage claim area when they spotted Emma standing there. As usual, she was surrounded by guys.

Eryn was about to call out to their friend when she felt Abi's hand on her arm. She looked to her right to see what the deal was when she saw Abi stop and stare.

She turned her eyes back to see Emma standing there with a different guy. She assumed it was the mysterious Braedon and was going to comment when she saw him kiss Emma.

The three of them watched the kiss and Eryn felt a flip in her stomach that had nothing to do with the baby growing inside her. It was the kind of kiss that a man gave you when he was crazy about you. At least that's the way it felt when Chase kissed her.

"Did you see what I just saw?" Eryn asked to no one in particular.

Chase held his hand to his wife's back, "Yep," he answered with a smile.

Abi shook herself mentally and said, "Oh yeah."

They watched the man walk away from Emma and figured the coast was clear.

Eryn called out, "Emma!" and waved.

Emma saw her friends and was relieved. She didn't know what the hell was going on and she needed the welcomed distraction of something familiar.

Walking quickly, she made her way over to where Abi, Eryn, and Chase were.

"Hello there," she said loudly.

There were hugs passed around and dry comments about marrying Russians and getting knocked up. Everyone laughed and made the expected snide responses.

After the initial greetings were done, Abi asked, "Where's Braedon?"

Emma looked behind her and, seeing him on his phone, frowned.

"He's over there," she said to her friends.

They all started to walk over to where Braedon stood.

Braedon left a message on his brother's voicemail, "It's me, made it to Philadelphia. I'll call sometime this weekend."

After he hung up, he saw Emma coming toward him followed by three people.

Given the descriptions she gave, he figured this was the group from MCAS Kaneohe Bay.

"Braedon," Emma said as she came up to him and wrapped her arms around one of his, "these are my friends, Abi Rochelle and Eryn and Chase Johnson."

Smiling, Braedon stuck his hand out to shake Chase's first. Then he stepped forward to give both Abi and Eryn a quick peck on the cheek.

Emma wanted to roll her eyes at the dreamy looks her friends had on their faces.

Chase spoke first, "Good to meet you, Braedon. We've heard nothing about you."

Laughing, Eryn playfully swatted her husband's arm. Of course, he was right.

"She's been tight-lipped," Abi chimed in.

Braedon looked over at Emma and smiled before saying, "Really?"

Eryn nodded, "Yes, and we were very demanding."

Feeling uncomfortable, Emma clapped her hands together and said, "Well, now that I'm feeling trapped, let's get in the car and go to Delaware."

Amidst laughter, the group made their way over to the rental car counter.

The ladies decided weeks ago to get a van so everyone could ride down and back together. Chase grumbled the whole time he was signing the contract and his wife was giving him the "stop it" look.

Braedon watched the friends and thought they were very nice people. He could tell that the women were friends from way back just by their easiness with one another. It was enviable to have friends like that, friends that would travel cross country to share your joys.

"Ready," Chase said loudly and motioned for everyone to follow him.

They walked out and got into a shuttle to take them to where the rental cars were parked.

Everyone got into the van, the girls choosing to sit together in the back seat so they could talk. Braedon sat in the front passenger seat while Chase drove.

It was evening so the traffic wasn't great, but Braedon figured it could definitely have been worse.

Chase drove them down Interstate 95 into Delaware and then got onto Highway 1. The drive was actually pretty and Braedon didn't say much, choosing to watch the scenery.

"Not a big talker, huh?" Chase asked Braedon.

Looking over at Chase, Braedon smiled and responded, "Not much."

The steady stream of chatter from the girls filled the vehicle and Chase laughed and nodded back at them.

"You'd think they didn't talk at least once a week," Chase said dryly.

Braedon peeked back to see Emma putting her hand on Eryn's rounded belly and laughing at, what he assumed was, the baby kicking.

Smiling, Braedon said, "It's nice to be together, though."

Chase looked over quickly then back to the road before saying, "Wait until Mitch and Katherine are in the mix."

Sighing, Braedon wondered if he would feel like odd man out since he was the "new guy."

"Don't worry," Chase said, "Mitch and I will save you. We know how overwhelming this crew can be. Not to mention Mitch's family is very….energetic."

Nodding, Braedon listened quietly.

After a few minutes, Braedon asked Chase, "How long have you and Mitch known one another?"

Chase grimaced before answering, "About thirteen years now," he sighed then asked, "has it been that long?"

Understanding, Braedon smiled. It was easy to wake up and wonder where the years went. He'd done it a time or two himself.

"So you're a civilian contractor now?" Braedon asked him.

Chase nodded. "Yes," he said. "I couldn't be a Marine and be married to Eryn. She was my OIC."

Braedon grimaced and asked, "How did that happen?"

Glancing over, Chase stared at Emma's boyfriend. He was surprised she didn't give him the full story.

Sensing Chase's unspoken question, Braedon offered, "Emma gave me the gist of it but I was just being nosy."

Nodding, Chase smiled, "It just happened," he sighed, "One day it was like, yes, she's the one."

Hearing Chase's tone, Braedon found himself feeling envious of the other man's assuredness. He himself didn't think it would ever be that simple for him. No fireworks, no epiphany, no shot to the heart.

They spent the rest of the ride in silence. The low volume of music, combined with the girls' chatter, was enough.

It was past seven in the evening when the group made it to Mitch's family's home.

Chase barely stopped the vehicle when they saw people pouring out of the house. Mitch and Katherine were leading the group.

"The gang must all be here," Chase announced as he turned off the van.

Braedon got out and immediately opened the back door for the girls to file out of.

He stood aside and held his hand out for each of them, taking extra care with Eryn. When everyone was out, he shut the door and stood right by the van.

Emma was lucky, she hadn't met all of Mitch's family but she felt like she knew them through Eryn's descriptions and knew they were a boisterous bunch. Looking around, she didn't see Braedon right away.

"Welcome!" Aly, Mitch's mom yelled to everyone.

All at once, everyone was hugging and talking and it was a happy chaos.

After hugging Mitch and Katherine, Emma turned to see Braedon still by the van. She cocked her head and turned around to walk toward him.

"Are you okay?" she asked him.

Braedon nodded, "Yes," he said, "just giving everyone a moment to say hello."

She didn't buy his excuse but let it go.

Taking his arm into hers, she turned to start walking toward the house.

"Or maybe," Emma started, "you're just not comfortable with all these loud people."

Braedon smiled. "Maybe," he commented.

Emma shook her head but laughed.

They were walking up toward the house when Mitch and Katherine met them before they climbed the front porch steps.

"So, you're Braedon," Mitch said sternly, then stopped. "Not Braedon Richards?"

Focusing, Braedon started laughing. He answered Mitch's question with his own, "Not Mitch Frinnel?"

"Holy crap, man!" Mitch exclaimed and hugged Braedon.

The women stood there, looking shocked.

Finally, Braedon realized he and Mitch were the only two in on the joke.

"We were stationed together on the East Coast," he said to Emma.

Emma swiped at his arm, "Stop it!" she said loudly.

Katherine smiled and stepped forward, "Welcome, Braedon. I'm Katherine," she said warmly.

Braedon leaned over and kissed her cheek, then he turned to offer his hand to Mitch.

Taking the offered hand, Mitch smiled widely, "Welcome, Braedon."

The foursome went into the house and entered into more loud, noisy conversation.

Emma kept a tight grip on Braedon's arm. She felt like if she didn't keep the connection between them, he might bolt out the door.

Even with her own crazy family, Emma was a little overwhelmed by the Frinnel household.

Matt and Aly, Mitch's parents, were hosting the wedding at their home and invited everyone to stay there for the weekend.

Katherine's parents were flying into a closer, private airport and would arrive sometime this evening.

"Please," Matt Frinnel said loudly, "eat."

Everyone started to move toward a large table where food was set out for the group.

Braedon waited patiently for everyone to start getting plates and piling them up. The food looked delicious and everyone seemed nice, but he just liked to sit back and take it in before he jumped in.

He was relieved that he knew Mitch. They weren't buddies when they were stationed together, but they went out a few times to work functions and he respected Mitch as an asset to Crash, Fire, Rescue.

Emma stood next to Braedon and kept stealing glances at him. She wasn't sure what she expected him to do when they got here but she now found herself feeling worried about it.

Looking over at Emma as she bit her lip, Braedon smiled.

"It's okay, Emma. I'm fine," he whispered in her ear.

Smiling slowly, Emma looked over at him. His eyes were a beautiful greenish-brown. They reminded her of the color of the leaves in the fall. She started to feel very warm as she stood there looking into their depths.

Eryn stood with her husband and watched Emma with Braedon a few feet away. There was something so intense about the way they looked at one another. It wasn't difficult for Eryn to see that her friend was pretty confounded with this Marine.

"What are you smiling about?" Chase asked his wife.

Smiling, Eryn turned to look at her husband. Her heart did a little skip and then the baby kicked. It was still new and exciting every time the little one did that. She remembered a moment when she wasn't sure they would ever make it but here they were.

She nodded toward Emma and Braedon, "I'm watching my friend," she answered.

Nodding, Chase glanced over at the couple then looked back to his wife. He thought she was the most beautiful woman in the world.

"Ahhh, the mysterious Braedon," he said in a low voice.

Eryn play-punched his arm, "Stop it," she whispered sharply.

Putting up his arms, Chase chuckled, "Hey, I like the guy. I'm just surprised since he's not her usual type."

Her husband's comment earned him a sharp look.

"I'm not trying to insult Emma or Braedon," Chase said softly, "I'm just saying, he's…."

Eryn nodded and answered, "I know."

Mitch walked up to his Best Man and slapped him on the back.

Looking to Eryn and then to Chase, Mitch asked, "Why the serious looks?"

Blushing, Eryn cleared her throat. If Emma knew they were gossiping about her, she'd probably kick all their butts.

Chase nodded toward Emma and Braedon before saying, "We're just watching."

Nodding slowly, Mitch said, "He's a really nice guy."

"He is," Chase responded, "he's just not what we expected."

Mitch threw his head back and laughed. It was one of those belly laughs.

Everyone looked over and figured he was laughing at some joke his friend told him.

Chase frowned at his friend and asked him, "What was so funny about that?"

Slapping his friend on the shoulder, Mitch said, "Why are you so surprised? Did either of you think you'd end up together?" He pointed toward his lovely bride-to be, "Do you think I thought for one second I'd end up with that gorgeous woman over there?" Then he pointed toward Abi and Gav, and added, "Did we think for one milli-second Abi would be okay with a guy her parents picked out for her?"

Both Eryn and Chase looked at Katherine and then back to Mitch before they broke out in laughter.

It didn't matter that everyone else didn't get the reason, they knew that they were laughing at how lucky they all turned out to be.

Chapter 9

Everyone finally filed through and got their food. People were sitting in every available spot. Emma wound her way through the living room and into the family room that was empty. Most of the guests were concentrated near the dining room and kitchen so it was a little quieter here.

Braedon followed her silently.

He held out his hand to take her drink while she sat. Once she was settled on a couch, he gave it back to her. He sat beside her and started eating.

Emma was hungry only minutes earlier but now, she was almost nauseous. 'What's wrong with you?' she demanded of herself silently.

Picking at her food, she managed to get down a few bites but it was a pitiful effort.

Looking over, she noticed that Braedon had no such issues.

After washing down the delicious food with some water, Braedon looked over at Emma. Her head was tilted down, staring at her almost-full plate, and she was pushing the food around on it with her fork.

"You don't like it?" he asked.

Emma jumped at the sound of his voice. She was unnaturally preoccupied with her food and its position on her plate.

Trying to engage her mind, she smiled weakly and replied, "It's great."

Braedon nodded toward her plate, and said dryly, "All evidence to the contrary."

Rolling her eyes, Emma shook her head in exasperation. "It's fine, I'm just thinking," she practically snapped.

He took her plate from her and set it on a nearby table along with his. He sat back down next to her and leisurely put his arm along the back of the sofa. His hand happened to be near her hair so he absently played with the strands while he watched her.

Emma sat there and watched him watch her and grew more frustrated with each passing moment. Finally, she slapped at his hand and stood up.

"What's wrong?" Braedon asked her.

Feeling cornered was not a common thing for Emma. She didn't like feeling this out-of-control and she couldn't even explain why she felt that way. So, instead of using all her sense to talk it out, she exploded at Braedon.

She pointed at him, and yelled, "What are you doing?"

Clearly confused, Braedon frowned and answered, "I'm sitting here and watching you think."

"That's just it," Emma shouted, "don't do that!"

Katherine was doing the rounds when she heard a raised voice coming from the family room. When she walked into the room, she saw an upset Emma yelling at her boyfriend.

Katherine walked over and put her arm on Emma's shoulder before asking her, "Is everything okay here?"

Emma felt ashamed. She didn't yell and scream and shout and here she was, practically throwing a temper tantrum.

"I'm sorry, Katherine," she murmured to her friend.

Hugging Emma, Katherine answered, "It's okay."

It wasn't, but Katherine would never say that. Emma always seemed so in control. To see her like this was definitely an anomaly.

Braedon stood and smiled at Katherine, "I think we're just beat from the trip," he said and gently took Emma's arm. "Maybe we'll take a little walk and clear our heads."

Nodding, Katherine got the impression that Braedon was used to "handling" people. She wasn't sure if she liked that particular trait or not. She would, however, reserve judgment on him for the time being.

Emma sighed, but followed Braedon outside. Her behavior shamed her enough to give in and follow him. Normally she would have stood her ground and told him where to go.

They walked down the driveway and turned onto the main road.

Braedon didn't say anything as he walked and looked at the houses they passed. Each one was huge, with equally impressive yards. It was so nice to see space; the direct opposite of what he usually saw in San Diego. People there were almost on top of one another.

"What happened?" Emma asked.

Shaking his head, Braedon answered, "I don't know."

Surprised that she actually asked the question out loud, Emma blushed.

They walked a few more blocks before she stopped.

Facing him, Emma looked so confused.

He knew what she was thinking. She was thinking, 'What am I doing here with this guy?' Braedon wasn't so blind that he didn't see he wasn't even in the same universe as her.

She was champagne and he was cheap beer. She was caviar and he was crackers with cheese. But, even knowing that there was a gap between them socially, she was here with him and that was good enough for right now.

"You confuse me so much," Emma whispered.

Braedon cupped her cheek, he didn't know what to say to that.

As if she realized where they were and what they were there for, Emma shook herself physically and turned around.

She took Braedon's hand and said, "We'd better get back."

It took half the time to get back to Mitch's family home and the lights of the house shined like a beacon. They were still holding hands and Braedon found he liked the feel of her skin on his. It wasn't just a sexual thing, it was something else that he couldn't quite name yet.

"There you are!" Eryn shouted as they turned down the driveway. "We've been waiting on you to start the rehearsal."

Emma snarled and snapped a quick, "Sorry."

Blowing off Emma's moodiness was a part time job for Eryn. "No crap, Cantrell, get your butt in here," Eryn responded.

They walked into the house and it was a kind of controlled craziness.

There were people walking around with food but most everyone was filing out the back kitchen door.

Emma, Eryn, and Braedon followed the crowd and got outside to see the Reverend lining people up.

Nodding to Emma, Braedon let go of her hand so she could go up and stand in the appropriate spot for the wedding party attendees.

Emma was all the way to the left, so she would be the first one down the aisle. Next would be Abi, then Eryn, and then the bride.

For being five months pregnant, Katherine glowed and drifted down the aisle as if she were walking on a cloud of happiness. If it weren't for the fact that Emma adored her, she might be jealous.

Everyone was arranged and the rehearsal started.

Being the comedy relief with her acerbic barbs, Emma started in right away. "About time someone caught you, Frinnel."

Laughing, Mitch shouted out, "Your time is coming, Cantrell!"

Even though her friends were laughing, Emma stopped cold. Her eyes sought out Braedon and she apologized with them. She needed to remember that it wasn't just her who could get feelings hurt here.

The rehearsal started and all the guests quieted down.

It only took about fifteen minutes and then everyone was let go to get back to the festivities.

Emma looked for Braedon but couldn't find him.

"He went with the guys on some "guy" thing," Abi said from behind her.

Turning around, Emma was puzzled.

Swiping her hand, Abi said, "Oh don't worry, I'm sure they'll get him liquored up and leave him on some curbside brothel in town."

Emma snorted and snapped, "Nice."

Abi shrugged, "Just don't worry about the guys. We're going up to be with Katherine, you coming?"

Nodding, Emma followed Abi through the house and upstairs.

They went down a long hallway and came to a door that led up another flight of steps. Emma could hear giggling and followed Abi up.

When they came into the room, Emma gasped. It was like a room straight out of a fairy tale.

Eryn and Katherine were sitting on the bed, rubbing each other's bellies.

"Stop that!" Abi said sternly.

Sticking out her tongue, Eryn answered, "You're just jealous."

Abi nodded, "Probably," she said, "but my time will be here soon enough, I suppose."

Emma piped up, "That Russian going to give you lots of babies?"

Winking, Abi flopped down on an oversized pillow next to the bed, and replied, "Lord, I hope so," in a dreamy voice.

She couldn't help it, Emma rolled her eyes.

Sitting down on a nearby chair, Emma asked, "What happened to the clubs and the guys and all that stuff?"

Eryn looked at her friend Emma, then over at Abi, and finally at Katherine. When her gaze came back to Emma, she shrugged and said, "I have no idea."

All four of them laughed.

Emma was glad that her friend was honest. She supposed none of them really saw what was coming into their lives. The best they could hope for was it didn't hurt too much if it all went to hell.

Shaking herself mentally, Emma pushed those negative thoughts out. There was no use in thinking that when it came to her friends.

Watching the three of them talk and giggle, Emma knew she had the best kind of friends, the ones that stuck with you no matter what.

"A toast," Abi said, and handed Emma a glass of champagne. "Only sparkling cider for you two," she said to Eryn and Katherine.

Emma took the glass and raised it.

Abi cleared her throat and said, "To the men, the babies, and the love we've found with them and each other. May it never end."

"Here, here!" Emma shouted and took a long sip of her champagne.

A bottle of champagne later, the four of them were doubled over laughing. Of course, only Emma and Abi were drunk but their antics made Eryn and Katherine laugh even more.

"Okay," Katherine said, "spill it, Emma."

Knowing that her interrogation was going to start, Emma tried to look innocent. It was a bad act but she had to try.

Abi pushed into Emma with her shoulder, "Oh come on now; we want to know all about a certain Mr. Braedon." She drew out the words.

Rolling her eyes, Emma pushed Abi back, "We met when he picked me up for a party."

Katherine drew back in surprise, "You hadn't met him before then?"

Shaking her head no, Emma explained, "I was supposed to go with my friend Dave but he was running late. He asked Braedon to pick me up."

Eryn nodded and asked, "I've met Dave, right?"

Emma nodded, "Yes." She drank from her glass, "Anyway, Braedon never told me that the party we were going to was for him so I was pretty…."

The three of her friends looked at her and said in unison, "Emma."

All of them laughed.

Saluting her friends, Emma drank some more champagne. At least the liquid made her feel less stressed out about a certain Marine that she couldn't figure out.

"Now the good stuff," Eryn said, "that kiss in the airport, whew, I had to fan myself after seeing that."

Abi nodded in agreement, "I know, right?"

Katherine sighed, "I missed it."

Emma looked at each of them and turned a bright red.

Abi saw Emma's expression and laughed. "Oh my Lord," she exclaimed and asked, "is that embarrassment I see on your face, Emma Cantrell?"

The sting of being put on the spot was tough and Emma hoped Braedon was having a better time of it with the guys.

Chapter 10

Braedon sat at the bar and nursed his beer. He sort of assumed the role of DD when they got to the pub.

Down the bar, Mitch sat with Chase on one side and Braedon on the other. The two men were drinking heavily and Braedon suspected it was to calm nerves.

"Another!" Mitch shouted as he slammed his empty beer glass down on the bar.

Chase nodded to the bartender and then turned to face Braedon, "How are you doing?" he asked.

Nodding, Braedon answered, "Pretty good," then he asked Chase, "You?"

Slapping his new friend on the shoulder, Chase slurred out, "I'm fine, and it's him we have to worry about. He's nervous."

"Uh uh," Mitch said loudly, "I'm fine, you were the one who was nervous."

Chase took a gulp of beer, "No way!" he retorted.

Chuckling, Braedon watched the two friends bicker.

As if re-focusing, Chase looked over at Braedon, "Hey," he said, then asked, "What's the deal with you and Emma?"

Knowing the questions were coming and being asked them were two different things. Braedon felt a little panicked and thought honesty was the best policy.

"We met by accident," he answered.

Mitch's attention was focused on the story, "Really?" he asked.

Nodding, Braedon ordered a white soda and turned to face Chase and Mitch.

He nodded to the bartender and started, "Well, I gotta say, she's probably the most beautiful woman in the world."

Both men nodded.

"And I have absolutely no clue what she sees in me," he added.

Chase nodded again and said, "Holy crap, I think that about Eryn almost every day."

Mitch rubbed his hands down his face and said, "Me too. Katherine is this great person and what the hell is she doing with me?"

Braedon laughed. Obviously the alcohol brought up the insecurities. He was pretty sure, knowing what he did about Emma's friends, that these guys had to be pretty cool to make the cut.

"I'm sure," Braedon answered, "that the ladies see a bit of something in the both of you in order for you to be in their lives."

Chase nodded and said, "Too deep."

Laughing, Mitch picked up his beer mug, "Yep, Braedon," he slurred, "let's stick to sports or cars or something like that."

Picking up his glass of soda, Braedon said, "Okay, you got it."

A few minutes later, a man came into the pub and made his way over to where the three men sat at the bar.

Mitch saw him first and yelled out, "Gav!"

Chase turned around and stood up to give the man a hug.

Braedon remembered that this was Abi's fiancé from New York.

He was a good looking guy, Braedon thought; snazzy dresser too.

"I'm Gavriil Maslov," he introduced himself to Braedon.

Taking Gav's extended hand, Braedon said, "Braedon Richards."

Nodding, Gav asked, "Oh, Emma's guy, right?"

"Right," Braedon answered.

They sat back down at the bar and Gav ordered a beer.

A few minutes later, Gav turned and asked Braedon, "Are you a gambling man, Braedon?"

Looking at Gav, Braedon grinned, "Been known to be."

Feeling downright drunk, Emma practically slid down the stairs from the "castle room." She was giggling with Abi as they tried to make their way to their respective bedrooms.

"Shhh," Abi slurred.

Emma cupped her friend's mouth and said, "I know, you're the one being loud."

They got out into the hallway to find Mitch's mother, Aly, standing in the hallway with her hands on her hips.

'Busted,' Emma thought to herself.

"Are you two ladies looking for your rooms?" Aly Frinnel asked.

Not knowing what to do, the two of them just nodded.

Chuckling, Aly said, "Follow me."

Holding onto one another, Emma and Abi followed Mitch's mom.

"Abi, you and Gav will be in this room," Aly said as she stopped at one of the doors.

Abi hugged Emma and murmured, "G'night."

Emma watched her friend close the door and looked over to see Mitch's mom smiling. She smiled back and knew she looked ridiculous.

Taking Emma's arm, Aly said, "C'mon, princess, let's get you to bed."

She giggled at the endearment Mitch's mom used. It was one her dad used when she was little.

They stopped at the next room and Aly opened the door as she said, "I had Matt put your bags and Braedon's in here."

Emma was in the room, the door closed behind her, before she realized what Aly said. Holy crap! Braedon was in the room with her?

Panic set in. Pulling out her phone, she wanted to call someone but didn't know who to call.

She stood in the bedroom, staring straight ahead, and hoping she wouldn't make a complete fool of herself.

The guys came stumbling in about one in the morning. Braedon drove and was relieved they found their way back to the house since he was relying on a rather intoxicated Mitch to provide directions.

He helped the groom get up the front porch steps while Gav helped Chase up, although he wasn't in much better shape.

They opened the door to find Mitch's mother and father standing in the entryway looking at them.

It was like they were teenagers rather than grown men because all of them straightened up and acted like they'd been caught doing something bad.

Aly Frinnel was the first to crack a smile, "Okay, let's get the groom to bed before the bride sees what she'll have to live with for the rest of her days."

The guys laughed and Mitch grumbled.

Aly led Chase, Gav, and Braedon upstairs while Matt took his son's arm and led him toward the bedroom downstairs.

Braedon smiled while he helped get Chase and Gav upstairs. He was really glad he wouldn't have a hangover the next morning.

"Braedon, this is your stop," Aly Frinnel said when they came to the first door at the top of the stairs.

Danette Fogarty

Braedon let Gav take the rest of Chase's weight and nodded to Mitch's mom.

"Thank you," he said and smiled as the lovely woman led the two stumbling men down the hall.

He opened the door and went inside. The room was dark and he couldn't find a light switch anywhere around the door.

Crap! Walking slowly, Braedon made his way further into the room. He felt a door on his left and opened it up. Luckily, it was a bathroom. He flipped on the switch and squinted at the bright light.

He made quick work of brushing his teeth and getting ready for bed. Surprisingly, his toiletry bag was already in the bathroom.

Once he left the bathroom, Braedon looked around for his bag. He found it right outside the bathroom door and laid it down so he could open it.

Stripping off his clothes and tossing them into a pile, he rifled through his bag for his pajamas. He was pulling the shirt on over his head when he heard a familiar voice.

"Nice show," Emma purred.

Emma was sleeping in bed when she heard the door open and close. She could make out Braedon's form as he made his way into the bathroom. Sitting up, she watched him, backlit by the bathroom light, while he brushed his teeth and finger combed his short hair.

When she spoke, she saw him jump.

"Emma?" Braedon asked.

Smiling, Emma pulled her knees up to her chest.

She absently ran a hand down her own hair to make sure it wasn't sticking up before saying, "By your reaction and question, I'm assuming you didn't know we were sharing a room."

He couldn't make her out clearly since the bathroom light didn't make it all the way into the bedroom.

Clearing his throat, Braedon answered, "I didn't."

Emma was secretly glad he seemed as conflicted as she was about the situation.

She sat there on the bed for a long while, trying to figure out what to do. There was a small chair in the room, but neither of them would be comfortable sleeping in it. There was really no choice but to share the bed and, the more Emma thought about it, the more she liked the idea.

But, for the life of her, she couldn't figure out why....again.

"Uh," Braedon said as he backed up into the bathroom, his shorts in front of him like a shield.

He closed the door and could hear Emma's laughter follow him.

A minute later, he came out of the bathroom.

Emma was sitting in the bed, leaning up against the headboard, and looking very smug.

As he walked over, he could also see how gorgeous she was. Even without the makeup, her skin was flawless and looked tan.

Most women would look washed out by lamplight but not Emma.

Trying to contain his growing awareness, Braedon sat down on the edge of the bed.

"I know," Emma said before he spoke, "I was a little confused too."

Braedon nodded.

Emma patted the bed beside her and said, "No use being a gentleman and offering to sleep on the floor or in the chair. I'd be offended."

Smiling, Braedon slid onto the bed. He was careful not to touch Emma as he mimicked her position of sitting against the headboard.

It made him feel weird that she knew exactly what he would offer.

"I see this as an opportunity to get to know one another," Emma said and shifted so she was laying on her side and facing him.

Again, Braedon followed her lead and did the same.

Each of them lay there on the bed, smiling at each other.

Emma spoke first and asked, "How drunk are you?"

"Not bad," Braedon responded, then added, "I'm the one in the best shape."

Chuckling, Emma nodded, "I was pretty wasted earlier but we went to bed early." She sighed, "The price we pay for having two pregnant women in the wedding party."

Braedon smiled widely, "They tried to grill me but they were already pretty gone so it wasn't too bad."

Nodding, Emma played with the corner of her pillow.

She looked over and met his eyes with her own. Their green-brown depths seemed to draw her in. It made her think of the ocean, how its color was never really defined.

Watching Emma as she laid her hand down on the bed between them, Braedon put his on the bed so it was just lightly brushing against the edge of hers.

The very small connection between them made Emma's heart flip.

They lay there in bed, their hands barely touching, and staring at one another.

Emma's eyes grew heavy and she knew sleep was pulling her into its embrace but she so wanted to stay up and stare into Braedon's eyes.

He had this sort of half smile on his face. It was as if lying here with her was the best thing in the world.

'How could any woman not feel a little special seeing that look on a man's face?' Was the last question to run through Emma's mind as sleep finally engulfed her.

Chapter 11

Emma woke up to her phone alarm going off. She reached out, without opening her arms to shut the damn thing off and her hand felt flesh.

Her eyes flying open, Emma looked over to see her hand on Braedon's cheek with his hand partially under it.

"I'm sorry," she mumbled as she sat up and turned to grab her phone off the nightstand.

Luckily Braedon woke up a while ago so when her arm swung out, he was able to put his hand up to soften the impact.

He stretched and said, "No problem."

Looking over at him, stretched out on the bed they shared, Emma watched him. He was long and lanky but still muscular. His body was definitely in shape, thanks to the stringent workouts the Corps mandated.

Feeling self-conscious, Emma ran her fingers through her hair to make sure it wasn't standing straight up.

"What's on the agenda for today?" Braedon asked as he sat up.

Emma was so preoccupied in watching Braedon that she had to jump start her brain. 'Geez,' she thought to herself, 'he's only a man.'

"Um," she finally answered, "we're supposed to meet for breakfast around nine and then the girls are going somewhere to have hair and makeup done."

Braedon reached over and swiped a strand of hair away from Emma's face. The motion surprised him in the fact that he did it without thinking.

Earlier, as he lay there watching her sleep, he wondered what it would be like, kissing her as if she belonged there, with him. Touching her in all the places he hoped would drive her crazy with want. Discovering all the little things he wanted to know about her. If the kiss in the airport was any indication, it would be like heaven on earth.

She also kept looking at him like he was some kind puzzle she couldn't figure out. It was very arousing but a little scary too.

"Do you want to use the bathroom before I go in there?" Emma asked.

She wished he would stop looking at her like that. It made her want to kiss him.

Sliding off the bed, Braedon nodded, "Sure," he said, "I'll be right out."

Once the bathroom door closed, Emma took a deep breath. What was wrong with her? This was stupid! They were here for the wedding. She needed to deal with that first and foremost.

An hour later, Emma emerged from the bathroom. She'd washed her hair and blow-dried it, but that was it. It was long and she didn't like having it hang loose like this but the hair dresser requested it. So she just brushed it until it was shining and smooth.

When she came out of the bathroom, she found Braedon talking on his cell phone. His back was turned to her so she quietly walked out of the room, wanting to give him privacy.

As soon as she went downstairs, Emma heard the noise. By the time she rounded the corner between the living room and dining room, it was like a dull roar.

There had to be twenty people in the room and everyone was trying to talk at once.

Emma looked around and managed to make eye contact with Abi, who waved her over to where she and Gav stood.

"Wow," Emma said as she came up beside her friends.

Abi nodded, "I know, right? They are all so……"

Gav answered, "Loud."

The three of them laughed.

Mitch saw them standing there and started to holler about getting the guests fed first.

Braedon hung up the phone with his brother and looked over to see the bathroom door open and Emma gone.

She either snuck out to avoid any further awkwardness or she was hungry and went downstairs.

Putting down his phone, he hoped it was the latter of the two.

When he got downstairs, Braedon saw there were people scattered around eating. He peeked into the different rooms, looking for Emma. There were a bunch of "Good Mornings," said and Braedon returned them with a smile.

He finally stumbled across the wedding party in the formal dining room. Chase was the first to spot him and stood up.

"Braedon," Chase announced, "our savior."

Leaning over, Braedon shook Chase's hand.

Mitch stood up next and leaned over, "Dude, you got us home in one piece," he said with a big smile.

Braedon nodded to Gav who waved but didn't stop eating. Abi was poking him in the side for his supposed rudeness. Eryn wasn't at the table and Emma was right in front of him so he put his hands on her shoulders and absently rubbed them.

Not expecting his touch, Emma jumped slightly when his hands started to massage her shoulders.

She knew he was in the room even before Chase said something. Maybe it was his cologne? 'Or maybe,' she said to herself, 'it's because you react to him when he's within ten feet of you.'

Abi was laughing at what the guys were saying about the previous evening's events. That was, until she happened to look over at Emma. Her friend, surprisingly, looked very uncomfortable.

"Okay," Abi announced, "Em, we need to get going to be with the bride." She motioned to the chair Emma was vacating, "Braedon, please have some breakfast with the guys."

Braedon kept standing until Emma and Abi left the room. Out of habit, he watched Emma leave. When he turned around, he found three sets of eyes on him.

None of the faces that went with those eyes were smiling and Braedon had the distinct feeling he'd done something wrong.

He sat down and smiled his thanks at Mitch's mom as she brought him a plate of food.

"What did you do?" Mitch asked Braedon once his mom left the room.

Looking confused, Braedon asked, "I'm sorry?"

Chase shook his head, "There is one thing you need to get straight, Braedon," he looked around to make sure none of the women were around, and added, "You piss off one of them, you piss off all of them."

Still wondering what they were talking about, Braedon frowned.

"It's clear," Gav added, "that he doesn't know what he did."

All three of his new friends shook their heads and looked at him like with pity in their eyes.

Putting up his hands, Braedon said, "I didn't do anything, I swear."

Gav sighed, "You better hope not."

The conversation turned to other topics and Braedon tried to keep up but he was desperately searching his mind for whatever he did to "piss off" Emma.

Abi was right on Emma's heels as they went upstairs.

She explained that Katherine wasn't allowed to see Mitch so she was eating breakfast with Eryn up in her room this morning.

They went up the second set of stairs and were well into the room when Abi let loose.

"What did he do?" Abi demanded to Emma.

Hearing Abi's tone, Eryn and Katherine stopped eating and stood to walk over to where Emma was standing.

Emma was not expecting the question and she didn't have an answer so she just stood there and shrugged.

Eryn spoke up and asked, "Abi, would you mind bringing the rest of us up to date?"

Pointing at Emma, Abi said, "Well, she seemed fine but as soon as Braedon came downstairs and put his hands on her shoulders, she jumped."

Emma looked around at the three women she loved the most in the world and wanted to laugh for the shocked look on their faces.

"Uh, What!" she said loudly.

Eryn stepped up and inspected Emma like she was an alien.

It was almost comical but it was also annoying.

Finally, Emma's defensiveness kicked in, "Look, it's Katherine and Mitch's wedding, we need to focus on that."

Katherine shook her head, "If I'm not mistaken, she looks a little flustered."

Eryn and Abi nodded in agreement. They were wearing dopey grins on their faces too, which only served to piss Emma off.

"Enough!" she yelled at her friends.

Turning around, she left the room and went down the stairs quickly, ignoring Eryn and Abi's pleas for her to come back.

She went to the room she and Braedon were "assigned to" and closed the door quickly.

Going into the bathroom, Emma splashed water on her face and tried to get her tumultuous feelings in check.

She was drying off her face with a hand towel when she heard someone come into the room.

Assuming it was Abi, Emma spat out, "I am not acting weird, and I'm fine; he's just a guy!"

Just then, Braedon came around the corner and stood in front of Emma.

"Really?" he asked her.

Oh, if the ground could open up and swallow her, she'd feel better.

Dropping the towel, Emma sighed, "I know it sounds strange, I'm sorry."

Grinning, Braedon leaned up against the doorjamb.

"Sounds very interesting," he said, then asked, "Care to enlighten me?"

Grumbling, Emma said, "No."

Braedon cocked his head, "Pity, I was just being told that I pissed you off."

Emma's head shot up, "Who the hell said that?"

He took her hand into his and pulled her from the bathroom into the bedroom.

"Okay," he said and had her sit on the bed, "you have to admit that your friends are going to get an opinion of what's going on between us so you need to just go with it."

His voice was calm and that only added to Emma's anxiety.

She shook her head and whined, "But there's nothing going on between us."

Braedon bit his lip to keep from laughing at her actions. She was acting like a child and it was adorable.

He looked at her closely and asked, "What did you think they would say, Emma?" Going around her, he sat down next to her on the bed, "You show up with a guy that you've told them nothing about and you're sharing a room with him."

Emma jumped up and paced in front of him.

"But we're not sleeping TOGETHER," she said while emphasizing the last word.

Braedon stood, walked up to her, and brushed the tip of her nose with his finger, "Aren't we, though?" he asked and walked out of the room.

'Dammit!' Emma yelled to herself.

After taking some deep breaths, she left the room and re-joined her friends upstairs. Before any of them could say anything, she plopped down on the bed and started talking.

"We're not together," she started.

Eryn stopped getting stuff together for the hair appointment and sat down next to Katherine. Abi was on the bed next to Emma.

Looking at her friends, Emma felt awful, "He's here as a companion of sorts," she said.

"Companion?" Abi asked.

Emma nodded and whispered, "I just didn't want to be the only one who was alone."

Katherine wanted to cry for her friend. Of course, she'd only known Emma for a couple of years since she knew her through Eryn but she'd grown to love Emma and Abi like sisters she never had.

Walking up to Emma, Katherine cupped her cheek, "You're never alone; we're all here together."

"Amen to that," Abi chimed in and all the women hugged tightly.

After they let go, Emma said lightly, "Let's forget all this boy stuff and get Katherine ready to get married."

Amidst laughter, the four friends went downstairs. Abi and Emma were the spotters to make sure that Mitch was nowhere in sight as they got Katherine out to the car and on her way to the salon.

An hour later, Emma was in a hairdresser's chair getting her hair done, with a glass of wine in one hand, and a beautiful hair piece in the other.

Katherine surprised the three of them with delicate hair pieces she felt matched their individual styles.

Emma's was intricately done in silver with brightly colored flowers. "Bold but lovely," Is what Katherine told her.

As soon as she blabbed about Braedon, they all seemed to calm down. It was like a load of weight was lifted off of her chest and Emma sure did like that.

She did, however, keep replaying the conversation she and Braedon shared in their room.

She absolutely hated the fact that he had a point.

Looking over, Emma was going to ask Abi about it when there was a commotion at the front of the salon.

Katherine's mother and father arrived and they were fussing over their daughter.

Anything Emma needed to say could be said later. Right now, they were celebrating family and that was far more important.

Chapter 12

The ceremony was scheduled for 3pm and at 2:50 the ladies were lining up to go down the aisle.

Katherine's parents insisted on a humongous tent that could seat almost two hundred. It was heated and back lit with thousands of little white lights.

The ladies' dresses were done in silver with different colored accents. Katherine designed them herself and had her seamstresses custom make them for Eryn, Abi, and Emma.

The three of them were oohing and ahhing over their dresses when they spotted Katherine and her father coming toward them.

"I'm going to cry," Eryn sniffled.

Abi hugged her arm and said, "No you won't, it will make your makeup run."

Nodding, Eryn dabbed her eyes with a tissue, "You're right," she sighed, "got it."

Emma smiled at her friends and thought they were the best. When she looked over to see Katherine coming toward them, her breath literally caught in her throat.

Katherine was a vision, in every sense of the word.

Emma couldn't remember any bride looking as gorgeous as Katherine did just then.

She looked over at Abi and Eryn, who were holding back their own emotions, and then back to Katherine.

Her delicate facial features were highlighted with muted makeup while her body was enmeshed into the most beautiful gown.

It was a cream colored material that was fitted around Katherine's chest and arms. There was a beaded and crystal-encrusted belt that fell just below Katherine's chest. The fabric then flared out into folds of cream that fell to the floor and shimmered as Katherine moved.

"She looks like something out of a Jane Austen novel," Emma whispered.

Abi nodded greedily, "Yes, she does, doesn't she?"

Eryn held her hand to her neck and couldn't seem to speak.

Once Katherine reached the three of them, she smiled big and made a face.

The totally unexpected reaction made all four of them giggle like school girls.

"You guys looked very serious," Katherine whispered to them as they gathered around in a circle.

"We were just kicked onto our butts by your beauty," Emma said.

Abi and Eryn nodded in agreement.

Spinning around, Katherine's dress whooshed quietly as the fabric settled around her.

She looked at Eryn and asked, "What do you think?"

Eryn shook her head and managed to choke out, "Oh my Lord, Katie, you are an angel."

Marcus Fredricks came up beside his daughter and cleared his throat.

"Katherine," he said in an emotionally choked up voice, "we need to get started."

Eryn couldn't ever remember seeing her uncle look so lost. She imagined that's what her dad looked like when she was about to walk down the aisle to marry Chase.

Nodding to her cousin, Eryn gave her a quick hug and motioned for Abi and Emma to get into place.

Braedon was seated behind the bride's mother, Victoria Fredricks, and he had no idea why.

Aly Frinnel had asked him to help the ushers if they ran into problems and they seemed to have it all in hand so he just stood around for a while. Then she asked him to escort

Katherine's mother to her seat. He thought it was a little odd since he wasn't dressed in a tuxedo as the other wedding party members were, but he couldn't say no.

Mrs. Fredricks looked really nervous as he introduced himself and said he would be escorting her to her seat. She held on to his arm like it was a life raft. Once he got her to the seat, she looked up at him and asked if he would sit behind her.

Again, he couldn't really say no. She was a very nice lady and the request seemed simple enough.

Now, though, he was sitting next to Eryn's parents, General and Mrs. Fredricks.

Talk about a power kick to the gut, sitting next to a General was never included in Emma's little explanation of things. He'd have a word or two for her the next time they were alone.

Beverly Fredricks leaned over and said, "I hear you're Emma's escort, Braedon. Is that right?"

"Yes, ma'am," Braedon said stiffly.

Tom Fredricks nodded and extended his hand, "Tom," he said.

The General just set the tone and it helped ease Braedon's nervousness.

"Sir," he said and shook Tom's hand.

Shaking his head, Tom said, "Not tonight, Braedon, it's just Tom."

Nodding, Braedon said, "Then, Tom," he said the other man's name pointedly, "you won't mind if I ask your lovely wife for a dance or two."

The expression on the General's face was priceless.

Beverly Fredricks laughed and winked at Braedon before saying, "I'd love to."

The music started so the guests quieted down.

Emma went down the aisle first. She had a hard time focusing when she wanted to look around and see the decorations. It was like walking into a fairytale. The aisle itself was lined with greenery. There were lights everywhere that glittered in the late afternoon light.

She focused on getting down the walkway without tripping or anything as equally embarrassing.

When she was almost to the front of the rows of guests, Emma finally saw Braedon. He was sitting next to Eryn's parents and that surprised Emma.

Not to mention, he looked like a movie star in the suit he was wearing. Seeing him look like that made Emma's heart speed up.

Braedon saw Emma and smiled. She was beautiful, and floated down the aisle.

Even when the other attendants, and then the bride, came down the aisle, his focus didn't leave Emma.

Everyone stood at the front of the tent, where blooming flowers emitted a wonderful aroma. The music changed and faded and then the Reverend started to speak.

Emma watched Mitch and Katherine and tried to hold back the tears. The ceremony was simple, they spoke traditional vows and lit the unity candle. It was only at the end of the ceremony when things got a little interesting.

The Reverend announced that they were man and wife and told them they could kiss.

Both Katherine and Mitch kissed quickly then Mitch lifted his wife up in his arms and made a beeline down the aisle.

It happened so fast that the rest of them had to run to keep up.

Everyone laughed at the chaos of it all and that started the party.

As the guests moved to greet the wedding party, the caterers rearranged the chairs to surround the tables for the dinner and reception.

The bride, groom, and their attendants were shuffled inside to get some pictures done while cocktails were served to the guests.

Beverly Fredricks wrapped her arm around Braedon's and walked with him over to the bar. Her husband was busy talking with Marcus and Victoria.

"So, what did you think of the ceremony?" she asked Braedon as she grabbed a glass of champagne.

Braedon smiled and answered, "It was lovely, ma'am."

Nodding, Beverly took a sip of her champagne before commenting, "I'm surprised that you noticed with your focus being on Emma."

Her comment made Braedon choke on his champagne. He wasn't expecting it. Of course, he suspected that Mrs. Fredricks was a woman full of surprises.

Rubbing Braedon's back, Beverly chuckled, "Caught you," she said slyly then moved over to talk to her husband.

Braedon shook his head slowly and walked toward where the wedding party went, a smile plastered on his face.

Emma was tired of smiling.

They posed for a ton of pictures and it was wearing her patience thin.

"Almost done," the photographer announced.

Glaring at him, since this was like the tenth time he said it, Emma clenched her jaw.

Abi laughed and murmured to Emma, "First drink is on me."

Emma rolled her eyes, "Considering it's an open bar, I doubt it," she said dryly.

They were about to throttle the photographer when, a few minutes later, he announced that they were done.

Eryn rubbed her back and said, "Thank goodness."

"Honestly," Emma started, "did the man not know he was dealing with a bunch of Marines?" She glared at the photographer and spat out, "We could kill him and nobody would know about it."

Mitch added, "Or at least they wouldn't find the body."

Chase nodded and said, "Or identify it."

"Nice wedding discussion," Katherine said.

Abi grabbed Gav's arm and shouted, "Okay, let's party!"

The group was heading toward the reception when they saw Braedon.

Leaning over toward Emma, Abi commented, "I'll tell you one thing," she sighed, "he is one fine looking man in that suit."

"I was thinking that myself," Emma replied and winked at her friend.

Now that the girls knew the score, Emma felt a little better about joking when it came to Braedon.

Braedon shook Mitch's hand and kissed Katherine's cheek in congratulations. He nodded to Eryn, Chase, Abi, and Gav before he came to Emma.

"Hello there," he whispered and leaned over to kiss her cheek.

Even though the kiss was meant as a sweet gesture, Emma reveled in the way it made her insides feel.

He stepped away and offered his arm for her to take.

Emma walked into the reception and felt lighthearted. Braedon was beside her, smiling. At that moment, it all seemed so right.

The group made their way to the head table, saying hi to guests as they went.

Danette Fogarty

Katherine and Mitch arrived first and sat down. The other couples found their seats. It was nice that even though Braedon wasn't in the wedding party, he was asked to sit at the head table as Emma's date.

The DJ started playing some jazz music and that was the cue for the guests to be seated for the dinner.

"You look lovely," Braedon whispered to Emma as he helped her get seated.

Looking up at him, Emma mouthed a 'thank you,' then waited for him to join her.

The food was served right away and tasted wonderful. Everyone ate and talked and laughed about the ceremony and their antics afterwards. The conversation flowed easily.

Braedon watched and listened to Emma and her friends and was, once again, touched by the affection they showed one another. He learned Gav was the newest member of "the club," having only proposed to Abi a few months earlier.

The guys were pretty clear that the ladies ran the show since they were the long-time friends, but, so far, the guys really liked one another too.

Chapter 13

After dinner was served and cleared away, the DJ announced the wedding party and invited the bride and groom out for their first dance.

Braedon watched as Mitch took his bride into his arms and masterfully danced her around the floor.

"Quite impressive, isn't he?" Emma asked him as they watched Mitch and Katherine.

Braedon nodded, "Yes, he is."

Emma leaned over and said, "His mother told me that the one thing she demanded of her boys was that they learn how to properly dance with a woman."

Nodding again, Braedon answered, "Mission accomplished."

Emma threw her head back and laughed. Without thinking about it, she moved her hand over so it covered Braedon's.

He looked over at her and smiled. If she wanted to touch him, he wasn't going to complain. Not one bit.

They announced that the wedding party would have the next dance so he expected Emma to dance with her escort, Mitch's brother. Instead she got up and offered her hand to him.

He was not going to turn her down.

They walked out to the floor and, although he didn't possess as much flare as Mitch in the dancing department, he was no slouch. He took Emma into his arms and started steering them around the dance floor.

This was heaven! Emma was sure of it. They were floating around the dance floor as if they'd been dancing together for years.

She allowed Braedon to take her anywhere he wanted to while they were dancing. There was something about a man who commanded the sheer physical complexities of dancing that was very erotic.

Emma looked up into his intense eyes and couldn't speak. She just let him lead her.

He held her close, one hand holding her lower back and the other gently cupping her hand in it. When they moved, the guiding hand on her back would move, causing his fingers to move. The friction of her dress against her skin, combined with the warmth from his hand, gave Emma a new zing of awareness. Now, for some reason, it felt like she was letting him lead her in more than just a dance.

Feeling uncomfortable, Emma waited until the song was almost over before dropping her hand from Braedon's shoulder.

She smiled weakly at the questioning look he gave her and said, "I just need to use the powder room."

Without waiting for his reply, Emma left the dance floor and made her way to the safety to the house.

Smiling at guests as she went, Emma just kept making a beeline for their room and the privacy it would give her.

After having to stop for greetings from several of Mitch's family members, Emma finally made it upstairs. She closed the door behind her and breathed a sigh of relief.

The only light in the room was cast from a small lamp in the corner. Most of the room was in shadow and that, for some reason, gave Emma a sense of comfort.

Why was this so confusing? Why was Braedon so confusing? This was supposed to be so easy. They were supposed to just come here so she wouldn't be alone. And now, after that kiss at the airport, she was all tangled up over him and didn't know what to do.

A few minutes later, Emma was still sitting in the room when she heard a soft knock on the door.

"Just a minute," she said quickly before walking over to open the door.

Thinking it was a lost guest, she pasted the obligatory smile on her face and opened the door, only to come face to face with Eryn's father, General Tom Fredricks.

"Mr. Fredricks," Emma said, trying to compose herself.

Tom nodded and said, "Emma, I am asking you to come back down to the reception with me, please."

The first thing Emma thought was, 'Something's wrong with Eryn,' so she nodded and stepped out into the hallway to follow Mr. Fredricks.

Without speaking, Tom Fredricks guided Emma downstairs and out the back door to the reception tent.

The look on his face made Emma worry as they walked into the tent. Tom pointed toward the dance floor, his eyes slit in aggravation.

"There," he said to Emma, "your date is monopolizing my wife."

Emma was so surprised by the words that she snorted while trying to keep from laughing.

She recovered quickly and said, "Uh sir," she cleared her throat, "I'm not sure I can help you with that."

Tom turned toward Emma, frustration showing clearly on his face. "Emma, you are a gorgeous, young woman. Keep him away from my wife."

It was too tough, Emma chuckled. The absolute look of agony shone on his face and Emma felt sorry for him.

She leaned over and kissed him on the cheek before saying, "I'll take care of it, sir."

Tom smiled his thanks and motioned for her to 'get to it.'

Moving around the edge of the dance floor, Emma was laughing. She couldn't believe the absurdity of the situation.

She kept one eye on Braedon and Mrs. Fredricks while she made her way toward them. They really looked like they were having fun and it was almost a pity to break it up. Almost.

The song ended and Emma moved in towards the couple.

"Okay," she said to Mrs. Fredricks, "I need him back now, ma'am."

Looking disappointed, Beverly Fredricks nodded. "Okay," she said to Emma then looked over at Braedon, "But later we'll dance again."

It wasn't a question but a statement of fact that made Braedon smile.

"Of course," he answered and smiled as she left him and Emma and made her way back to her husband.

Braedon finally looked over at Emma and found his stomach doing somersaults again at the sight of her. She was beautiful with her shimmering dress and heels that gave her legs more length. He longed to run his fingers across her skin and see just how long they were. Instead, he took her into his arms as the next song started.

"Where did you go?" Braedon asked her as they gently swayed to the music.

Pasting a smile on her face, Emma just shook her head and said, "Just checked on stuff inside the house."

It wasn't a complete lie but enough of one to make Emma feel guilty.

Feeling a bit prickly, she said, "You didn't seem to notice since your dance card was filled."

'Okay,' Braedon thought to himself, 'I hit a nerve.'

Gently rubbing her back, he leaned closer and whispered, "Were you lonely?"

Emma rolled her eyes, "No, but you were doing a good job of pissing off the General there," she nodded toward where Eryn's parents stood.

Braedon sighed, "We were just dancing," he said with a guilty smile on his face.

Now it was Emma's turn to push a button.

She pressed a little closer to him and said, "That's what you say but the General happened to think you were moving in on his territory."

Blushing, Braedon steered them away from where General and Mrs. Fredricks were standing.

Emma was having fun in teasing him so she pushed a little more, "You shouldn't move in on his territory you know, even Generals get a little jealous."

"Really?" Braedon asked.

He knew she was baiting him and, for the most part, he didn't mind it. There was something of a bite in her tone though and it made him wonder if the General wasn't the only jealous one.

Nodding, Emma let him lead her around to the music. It was a semi-slow song so they were moving faster with people weaving in and out around them.

The song ended and they broke apart, with Emma standing there and staring at Braedon.

Braedon allowed her to look at him, but it made him feel a little nervous.

Her eyes sparkled in the dimmed light of the tent. She simply stood there and looked at him again as if he was a puzzle she couldn't figure out. The words, 'Back at you,' stuck in his head.

The next song started and it was a slow one. Couples were gathering on the floor and swaying around them. Maybe it was the music, maybe it was the occasion, hell, maybe it was just the fact that Emma was only a foot away from him. None of it mattered….all that mattered was his need to have her with him, against him, touching him.

Without thinking any more, Braedon acted on his need. He stepped forward, as if he was going to take her in his arms to dance, but instead, he ran his hands down her arms and bent his head lower to kiss her deeply.

Emma only saw what Braedon's intentions were when it was too late to move away. That was if she actually believed she had the option to do so.

Once he was close, she felt heat rush into her veins and her pulse increase tenfold.

"Braedon," she whispered and was enveloped into the kiss.

His lips moved over hers, sampling every millimeter of them. She tasted sweet and he wondered if she realized how potent her taste was.

Emma closed her eyes, not caring who saw them, and ran her hands up Braedon's arms and held his head to hers. Her mouth opened at his insistence and her tongue matched his, thrust for thrust.

Kissing him was like drinking water after months of thirst; seeing a sunset after being in the dark for too long; feeling warmth after an eternity of winter.

The feelings overwhelmed her and made her feel small and fragile but also strong and brave. The contradiction was making her hate it and love it all at the same time.

Braedon tore his lips from Emma's and looked down at her. His chest was heaving from lack of oxygen and an overwhelming lust that burned his insides.

"How do you do that?" he asked her breathlessly.

Emma stared at him in wonder, "Do what?" she asked in return.

He gulped in air and swallowed hard, "Make me feel...." he couldn't finish the thought. No word seemed adequate.

"I know," she answered him and stepped away.

Before she could say anything else, Emma turned and walked off the dance floor. She left a confused Braedon standing there, staring after her.

Eryn, Abi, and Katherine stood at the far end of the dance floor and watched the interplay between Emma and Braedon, silly smiles pasted on their faces.

"Oh she has no idea," Eryn spoke first.

Abi shook her head, "I feel kind of bad for her, actually."

Katherine smiled, "Oh, how the mighty have fallen."

Their guys joined them.

"What's up?" Chase asked, knowing his wife was probably plotting.

Gav and Mitch exchanged glances. They figured that the girls were in on something.

Eryn smiled at her husband as his hand rested on her rounded belly. She would never get tired of feeling him touching her.

She looked at the men and asked, "You guys like Braedon, right?"

The three of them nodded.

"Good," she said, then turned to her friends, "we've got stuff to do, ladies."

The guys just smiled, knowing it was probably better that they didn't know the details.

Chapter 14

Emma went into the house and literally ran into Aly Frinnel.

"Whoa," Aly said smiling.

Feeling even sillier, Emma tried to brush it off with, "I'm sorry, I wasn't looking where I was going."

It wasn't difficult to see Emma was upset and Aly never let her kids get away without talking things out. Emma was a friend of Mitch's and Katherine's so she was a kid by association.

Gently taking Emma's arm, Aly turned and guided her into the living room that was currently empty. She sat down on the sofa bringing Emma with her.

"Now," Aly started, "what's going on?"

Looking at Mitch's mother, Emma was amazed. They didn't know one another all that well and Aly didn't know about the "arrangement" between Emma and Braedon so it was complicated. Knowing all that, Emma still felt the need to spill her guts.

Feeling nervous, Emma played absently with the hem of her dress and tried to come up with the words.

"Must be a man," Aly stated directly, "and since the man with you is Braedon, I'm going to assume it's him."

Emma's head shot up and she nodded.

"From the look on your face," Aly sighed, "he either hurt you or confused you."

Did the woman have ESP? Emma smiled slowly.

Nodding in return, Aly said, "Listen, I don't know all the details as it's really none of my business, but...." she took a breath before continuing to say, "There's only been one man in my life who made me feel crazy, happy, confused, mad as hell, and every other thing you can put a name to."

Wanting to know what Aly did about him, Emma looked over and asked, "What did you do about him?"

Aly smiled. It was one of those slow smiles that transformed her face into a bright and soothing picture.

"Simple," Aly said, "I married him."

Emma's chin dropped. Really?????

Patting Emma's hand, Aly chuckled. "Not the pearls of wisdom you expected, was it?"

Shaking her head, Emma laughed, "Not exactly."

"There are two choices in life, Emma," Aly said, her face growing serious now. "You can sit back and let it pass you by or take whatever love and happiness you can."

'Aha!' Emma thought. That's what she expected from Mitch's mom.

"Good Advice, Mrs. Frinnel," Emma said and leaned over to kiss Mitch's mom on the cheek.

Looking at Emma, Aly shook her head, "But not the advice you'll take right now, is it?"

Emma sighed but didn't answer.

Aly patted Emma's hand and stood, "Remember, Emma, sometimes we think there's all the time in the world to find someone who gets us." She walked to the doorway and turned around to say, "And sometimes that person walks away and we're left with a hell of a lot of what ifs."

Leaving the room, Aly smiled. Sometimes she wondered how she survived the three kids she had and their friends. As she walked out the door and toward the reception tent, she saw her husband Matt and said to herself, 'That's why.'

Emma sat on the sofa for a while and thought about what Mrs. Frinnel said and what Braedon said. There was no way she could feel something for him, it was too soon.

Turning, Emma caught a glimpse of pictures that were hung on the wall of the room. She stood and walked over to them.

There, on the wall, was the story of Mitch's family.

Pictures of Matt and Aly Frinnel were in the center. It looked like they were newly dating or married. As the pictures spread out, there were pictures of the kids. Summers at the beach, recitals or concerts. They were each candid photos of the family.

Emma had pictures at her place. Some were of her family but most of them were of her friends. She smiled as she thought about her own "life in pictures." It was varied and lovely but it didn't include anyone special.

Not wanting to dwell on such a sad thought, Emma turned and went in search of her girls. Eryn, Abi, and Katherine would help her get out of this funk she was in.

Five minutes later, the four friends were seated at a table in the reception tent. Emma and Abi had glasses of champagne while Eryn and Katherine sipped their sparkling grape juice.

"I'm a little jealous that I can't partake in the champagne," Eryn said as she ran a hand across her belly, "but I know it's for this little one so it's worth it."

Emma reached over to place her hand on Eryn's rounded baby bump and sighed.

Eryn smiled and placed her hand over Emma's, "You probably won't feel anything yet. Chase is ticked off because he can't feel it."

Fascinated by the fact that there was a little person inside her friend, Emma smiled and asked, "What's it like?"

There was no mistaking the dreamy look that settled over Eryn's face.

"Oh my, there are no adequate words," she answered and looked over at Katherine, who looked the same way.

Abi scooted forward toward the others and said, "I'm not sure I want to have kids."

The three friends looked at her with surprise clearly showing on their faces.

Katherine reached over and clasped Abi's hand, "That's certainly your decision and none of us will judge you if you decide that's what you want," she sighed and smiled at the baby moving inside her, "but I'll just say that knowing you're carrying part of yourself and your husband inside you is pretty amazing."

Abi nodded to her friend and thought about it. She looked over to see Gav talking to one of the other wedding guests and thought about what their child might look like. Would he or she be tall like their father? Would the baby have his blue eyes or naturally wavy hair? She joked yesterday about lots of babies but now she wondered.

Emma watched Abi and wanted to giggle at the adoring expression she wore. There was no doubt in Emma's mind that her friend would be knitting baby booties within the next year.

This conversation was a little too intense for Emma to handle so she excused herself and went over to the bar. The champagne wasn't strong enough to suppress her feelings of panic at all the talk of marriage and babies. She was happy for her friends as long as they were happy and that's what counted.

"A drink, Emma?" Chase asked from behind her.

Nodding, Emma turned around and hugged him. She could see how much he loved Eryn and that carried a lot of clout in Emma's mind.

She nodded to him and said, "If you're buying."

Chase nodded a yes and ordered from the bartender.

"How's it going?" he asked Emma.

She leaned against the bar and said, "A lot of talk about weddings and babies."

It was clear to Chase that Emma never wished any unhappiness for anyone, the domesticated attitude was just not something she seemed really comfortable with.

He picked up the glass the bartender handed him and said, "Let's drink." He waited for her to grab hers and lift it, "To the Corps, to family, and to friends."

"Well said," Emma tapped her glass to his and tipped it up to swallow. The liquid had a kick as it passed her lips.

Chase slapped his glass down on the bar and motioned for two more. If anyone could keep up with him, it would be Emma.

Gav and Mitch found them a few minutes later and joined in with the toasts.

Eryn, Abi, and Katherine stayed at the table and watched the others at the bar, smiles on their faces.

"If she wasn't one of my best friends," Abi said, "I'd march over there and kick her ass!"

Laughing, Eryn answered, "Amen!"

Katherine leaned in and said, "Look at her, she's gorgeous and flirts but you can tell she maintains full control over them."

Abi nodded, "I tell you, she's the man whisperer."

A smile formed on Eryn's face when she looked over and noticed that Braedon noticed Emma's audience as well. She nudged Abi and nodded to where he stood.

"Except for that man," Eryn said brightly. "She's got nothing over on him."

Laughing, Abi raised her newly refilled glass of champagne and sipped it, "Oh, he's not completely immune to it; he's just got her pegged."

Danette Fogarty

Katherine laughed, and then grabbed Eryn's arm, "Oh, oh, look, he's going over!" she whispered excitedly.

Braedon had been standing by a group of guests and talking about the Marine Corps when his gaze settled on Emma. Even though he'd looked at her a hundred times already, he never seemed to tire of looking at her.

He'd already memorized the way her hair changed color depending on how the light hit it. How her eyes were just as chameleon-like. They were a beautiful blue but looked almost gray if she was riled up.

His hands ached to touch her soft skin; he remembered brushing his hand across her back earlier while they were dancing and the contact sent a jolt of crazy attraction rushing through him.

Now, he saw her with Chase, Gav, and Mitch and toasting and drinking like she didn't have a care in the world while he was standing here, sulking.

He was about to turn to leave the tent and stomp up to the bedroom when a woman stepped in front of him.

"Hello," she said, "Braedon, right?"

Braedon nodded and, out of politeness, took her hand in his for gentle handshake.

She blushed and said, "I'm Michelle. I'm a cousin of Mitch's and was wondering if you'd like to dance."

Braedon was always taught to treat women like ladies and never be impolite. He nodded and guided her onto the dance floor.

Emma was laughing at something Gav said when her eyes caught sight of Braedon on the dance floor with some woman. The swift kick of jealousy hit her straight on and was so forceful, that she felt like she was going to fall over.

Pointing to the dance floor, Emma asked, "Who's that dancing with Braedon?"

Mitch turned and smiled, "Oh, that's my cousin Michelle. She's a doll."

A myriad of words was going through Emma's mind and "doll" was not among them.

Trying to tamp down on her growing anger, Emma clenched her jaw.

Abi looked at Eryn and all but choked, "Did you see that?" she asked.

Eryn nodded, "Oh, hell yeah!"

Katherine asked, "What did I miss?"

Pointing to Braedon and Emma, Eryn smiled like a sated cat.

Emma excused herself from the guys and made her way onto the dance floor. She was a little surprised at the effect the alcohol was having on her. Almost unsteady, it took all of her wits to keep from weaving as she walked.

Reaching the couple, who were, by the way, laughing, she tapped the woman on the shoulder.

Braedon was dancing with the charming Michelle and they were laughing at some of the stories she was telling him about Mitch when she stopped. He looked over to see Emma standing on the other side of her.

"Uh," Emma said unceremoniously, "you're dancing with my date," she tilted her head and smiled, "and I'd like him back now."

Wanting to laugh, Braedon stood there and watched the exchange between the two women.

Michelle sighed, "I was only keeping him company since you were otherwise engaged." She nodded to the bar area where Chase, Gav, and Mitch stood.

'Oh,' Braedon thought, 'Michelle you are a lot more than I gave you credit for.'

Emma's smile faded. "I was, yes," she batted her eyes, "but now I'm available again to dance with Braedon. Thank you so much for keeping him company."

The ice dripping from her words did little to suppress her anger directed at this little twerp. Emma didn't want to have to punch her but, if she didn't friggin move, it might happen.

Out of nowhere, Mitch arrived at Emma's side.

"Michelle," he said brightly, "you promised me a dance, sweetie."

Nodding, Michelle turned and kissed Braedon on the cheek, then took Mitch's hand and let him lead her away.

Emma stood there and stared at the woman's back.

Braedon couldn't decide if he wanted to laugh or kiss her. Deciding that she wasn't ready for the kiss he wanted to give her and laughing wasn't a wise option, he decided to quietly take her into his arms.

Letting herself be pulled up against Braedon's body made all the anger at the interloper, Michelle, dissipate. It was replaced by an awareness she was having trouble deciphering.

"Remind me not to piss you off," he said in a playful voice.

Looking up at him, Emma's face grew serious. She didn't want words anymore.

She ran her hand up his shoulder to his neck and massaged it while saying, "It's a way to keep my want in check."

"Your want?" he asked.

Emma stopped dancing and stood there, looking up at him, "Yes, the fact that I want you."

All of the blood in his brain fled. It was re-directing to other parts of his body now. The feeling made him light headed.

Swallowing hard, Braedon asked her, "Are you sure?"

Leaning closer, Emma brought her lips to his. The contact between them exploded into a million bits of desire.

She slowly pulled her lips off of his and asked, "What do you think?"

Braedon didn't answer, he couldn't. He only took her hand and brought it to his lips, kissed it softly, then turned to lead her off the dance floor.

At the bar, Mitch stuck his hand out to Chase, "That's twenty bucks, friend."

Chase handed over the money and thought it was worth it if Emma was happy.

At the table, Eryn, Abi, and Katherine were giggling like little school girls.

"You go, Emma!" Abi yelled and raised her glass.

Eryn and Katherine tapped theirs in a toast.

Chapter 15

Emma followed Braedon through the tent and into the house. They didn't say anything, just held hands as he led the way. A few people stopped them in greeting and Emma smiled benignly and let him chat for a moment before continuing on.

Her stomach was starting to flip as they rounded the corner of the living room and started up the stairs toward the bedrooms.

Feeling such an overwhelming need for someone and taking that leap into intimacy was difficult. People assumed because she was considered "pretty" and had a lot of dates that she was easy and slept around. That was most definitely not the case but Emma didn't discuss her sex life.

They walked up the stairs and stopped at the top of the stairway.

Braedon knew that once they walked through the door to the bedroom, all bets were off. He wanted to be a gentleman and offer her a way out if that's what she wanted. He took her into his arms and leaned down to give her a kiss.

The kiss was soft and reassuring. It also made Emma's blood pressure go through the roof. Perhaps if he would've been rough or cajoled her with words of love, she might've decided she didn't want to go down this road. But he didn't do that; instead, he was sweet and considerate and she knew he was giving her the choice.

Braedon pulled his lips from hers and looked into her eyes. They looked dark gray and reminded him of a stormy sea.

"Yes," Emma whispered to him.

Braedon nodded and turned to lead her into the bedroom.

With the muted light inside the room, they were cast into shadow immediately. Braedon quietly shut the door behind her and turned her to face him. Running his hands up her arms, he could feel her skin tremble as his fingers skimmed it.

Emma was melting, inch by inch, into a puddle of madness. Feeling Braedon touch her skin, feeling his breath as it whispered across her cheek, made her feel everything at once.

He was leaning against the bedroom door with Emma facing him. The bed was only a few feet away, but it seemed like miles. It was impossible for him to release his physical hold on Emma just to cross the distance.

Leaning in, Braedon held Emma's face gently as he captured her lips.

They stood there, him leaning against the door, her leaning against him, and kissing as if it were their last moments on earth.

Emma finally pulled back just enough to look into Braedon's eyes. They were wild and reflected the minimal light the lamp in the room gave off.

"This will change things," she whispered.

Braedon knew it, but he couldn't stop wanting her. Instead of answering, he bent his head and began kissing her shoulder.

Letting her head fall back, Emma allowed him to explore her skin. She never realized before now how sensitive the skin in the hollow of her shoulder was. Or how she could be so aware of another person.

Responding to Braedon, Emma splayed her hands across the back of his head and held it to her.

Feeling the stirrings of an orgasm start deep in her belly, Emma snapped her body straight and backed away.

There was no way she could have that happen from a man kissing her skin! She was confused and couldn't think.

"Are you okay?" Braedon asked gently.

He didn't dare cover the small distance between them for fear of not letting her go. The touches between them were like torches being set to gasoline. It was consuming and powerful.

Nodding, Emma was gasping for breath. Only a minute earlier she was willing to make love with him, but now she was scared silly.

Braedon couldn't deny the physical and emotional pain her refusal would bring but he would never force himself on her. He would never hurt her, even if it meant physical agony on his part.

Emma stood there and stared at Braedon. She couldn't form the words she needed to say since her mind was filled with thoughts of his touches and his kisses.

She finally came up to the surface of consciousness and asked, "How do you do that?"

Not sure what she meant, Braedon asked, "How do I do what?" in return.

"How do you make me feel that way?" Emma asked in a harsh whisper.

He couldn't help it, Braedon smiled. Not because she was funny, but because he asked himself the very same question.

Stepping toward her, Braedon answered, "We make each other feel that way, Emma."

Danette Fogarty

His words created their own seduction in her mind. He looked at her openly, as if he had no secrets. Emma wondered how she could keep up with that. The truth was, she couldn't.

She saw Braedon take another step closer and started, "I feel overwhelmed," she sighed, "and I want you so much I can't see straight."

Braedon was no stranger to sex but it was still a pretty potent feeling to have a woman say the words. It only made him want her more.

"I know, baby," Braedon whispered as he closed the final bit of space between them. "I want you too."

Emma smiled, thinking it was silly to think that she was the only one who wanted this. Or that making love with him would make her change. All that mattered was being with him.

Running her hands up Braedon's arms, she found the collar and pulled off his jacket. It fell to the floor behind him. Next, she slowly pulled his tie loose, managing the task without ever losing eye contact with him.

Holding his arms on Emma's waist, he let her begin undressing him. He wanted to see what she wanted. Pleasing her was his top priority.

"What do you want?" he asked huskily.

The question surprised Emma. She couldn't ever remember a man asking her that. The answer wasn't easy either, with her thoughts scattered by passion.

She smiled and kept unbuttoning his shirt.

After a good minute, she looked up and said, "I want it all, Braedon," then she wanted to giggle at the shocked look on his face.

Wrapping his hand around the back of her head, Braedon pulled her to him and said, "I'll give it all to you, Emma," before crushing his lips against hers.

The stakes were just upped a hundred fold.

Emma surrendered control for the first time in her life. She matched his passion with her own, running her hands through his hair and tugging it to emphasize the sensations he created inside of her.

Braedon helped Emma get his shirt unbuttoned and taken off, the cuffs catching on his wrist for a moment before he yanked the fabric hurriedly off and threw it.

Stepping back a half step, Emma took in the sight of Braedon's bare chest. She saw it the night before but now she could touch it as she pleased.

"Hmmmm," Emma purred as her fingers ran up and down his muscular chest.

"Do you like feeling my chest?" Braedon asked, surprised at the sound of his course voice.

Nodding, Emma leaned in and kissed the skin just below Braedon's neck. She ran her hands down his sides and snagged the top of his pants with her fingertips.

Braedon covered Emma's hands with his.

He took a hand and tipped her chin upward until she was looking at him.

Smiling, Braedon said, "I've got more clothes off than you."

Chuckling, Emma nodded, "And that's the way I want it right now."

He couldn't argue with her since that's what he asked earlier. Not that he wanted to, feeling her hands on his body was magical and made him feel so exposed and yet so strong at the same time.

Her fingers returned to the front of his pants and undid the button. She reveled in the sound of the zipper being lowered. Her hand ran over the hardness beneath the fabric of his pants and that sent a quiver through her body.

Knowing his reaction to her was so primal, was her undoing.

Emma pushed Braedon's pants down until they pooled at his feet. Without speaking, she turned around and lifted her hair up, silently asking him to unzip her dress.

Going slowly, Braedon ran his fingers up her sides, partly in retaliation from her manipulations of his body only minutes earlier. Her skin was so soft and smelled like a flower garden.

His fingers traveled up her shoulders, unclasped the dress, and then unzipped it.

Again, the sound of the zipper made Emma's heart explode with anticipation. 'What a funny thing to find sexy?' she asked herself.

When Braedon had the zipper down, he peeled the fabric off of her shoulders slowly. He dared not look up, for fear he wouldn't be able to control his want for her. Instead, he focused on the small of her back, where the zipper ended.

Emma allowed Braedon to pull her dress off her shoulders and shimmied out of the silky fabric as quickly as she could. There was a built in bra so as the fabric slipped away, her breasts were now exposed to the coolness of the room. Her nipples reacted by tightening up even more.

Dropping her head back, she set her hair free by removing the hairpiece.

Braedon wanted to see her; her back, although very sexy and mesmerizing, was only one small part of the surprise that was Emma.

He slowly turned her around so they were face to face once again. The breath in his lungs disappeared the second his gaze fell on her.

She'd let her hair down and the locks fell partially over her shoulder to cover her breasts. Somehow, the fact that she was still somewhat covered up, made her even sexier.

"Gorgeous," Braedon said in a rushed voice.

Emma stood there in her panties and heels, feeling like a seductress. She lifted her hands and placed them on Braedon's shoulders while stepping closer so they were touching from lips to thighs.

The friction her skin created against his was Braedon's undoing. Before he could think about it, he lifted Emma up into his arms.

Braedon's movement was such a surprise that Emma yelped when she was hoisted into his arms.

Grabbing his neck, she held on for dear life, "You're going to throw your back out or something," she said half joking.

Looking into her eyes, Braedon answered dryly, "I don't think so. You weigh as much as a blooming rose on a spring day."

'Oh,' Emma thought to herself, 'Southern boys sure do know how to make a woman feel good.'

Blushing, she could only shake her head in amusement.

Braedon carried Emma over to the bed and gently laid her on top of the comforter.

Emma sunk down into the softness and scooted over so he could lay down beside her. She frowned when he just sat on the edge and stared at her.

"What's wrong?" she asked him.

Braedon smiled slowly, and answered, "I want to find out your secrets and show you how a woman should be made love to."

Gasping, Emma lay there, propped up on her elbows and looked at his beautiful face. She could see want, that was obvious, but there was something else there as well. Whatever it was, it made her suddenly nervous about whether she would be able to make the experience good for him. She'd never doubted herself in this way before and it scared her.

Watching the emotions travel across Emma's features, Braedon realized she didn't know what to say to his words.

She didn't have to say anything; she only had to take the ride with him.

He lifted a hand and placed it over hers before saying, "Why don't we figure each other out, then."

Without any more words, Braedon moved so he was laying on the bed beside her. Her long, silky, hair was now moved behind her shoulders so her breasts were exposed for him. He placed his lips on her left breast, kissing it and encouraging Emma to relax into their lovemaking.

When the bud of dark rose was taut, he leaned over and took the other nipple into his mouth, giving it the same attention. His hands moved down her thighs, relishing in the softness of her skin.

After he was sure she was ready, Braedon moved so he was over her body. She wrapped her legs around the back of his, silently inviting him to love her.

Poised above her, Braedon closed his eyes for only a moment and pleaded for patience. He knew once he'd had Emma in this way, no other woman would ever be enough.

Emma lay beneath Braedon, caught up in her own pleasure, and trying to decipher the look on his face. He seemed to be concentrating on something but she didn't know what.

Feeling anxious, she said, "Love me, Braedon," through clenched teeth. "Please," she added.

Braedon adjusted his body so his hardness was pressed up against her warmth. He hesitated for a split second and then guided himself into her soft core.

As soon as Emma felt Braedon enter her, she moaned. It was like she'd been waiting for this one moment forever.

He stopped for a few seconds once he was inside of Emma, he had to or it would all be over. He needed to please her.

Looking into her eyes, Braedon concentrated on the sensations he could give her and began moving in long, slow strokes.

Feeling him moving in and out of her was like starting a riot of feelings. She didn't speak, only watched him watching her. Her body was screaming for more so she tightened her legs and moved her hips faster to meet his.

Emma set the pace and he wouldn't disappoint her. Braedon moved faster, smiling at the look of desire he saw in her eyes.

Before long, Emma found her orgasm was clawing at her, she arched up and dug her fingernails into Braedon's arms.

"It's too soon!" she yelled out.

Braedon smirked, "No, baby, it's not, just let it happen," he said, and thrust into her harder.

It was if he was reaching into her soul and pulling out everything she had. Emma couldn't hold back and arched up one final time, yelling out.

Not stopping, Braedon knew he was only moments behind her so he cupped her cheek with one hand as he thrust into her once more. He felt his insides turn to jelly as his climax crashed down through his body.

He knew he wouldn't be able to hold himself above her as he was sapped of all strength, so he lowered himself and rolled so she was now on top of him. They were still joined and he guided her head down so she was resting on his chest.

Tears streamed down Emma's face and onto his chest. She would be embarrassed later, but for now, she was just devoid of any strength.

They laid there for several minutes and would've stayed there all night except for the pounding on the door.

"Cantrell!" Eryn yelled from the other side, "I know what you two are up to and that's fine but the bride wants to throw her bouquet so get on clothes and get downstairs."

Emma and Braedon looked at one another for a second before starting to laugh.

Chapter 16

Ten minutes later, Emma and Braedon made their way downstairs to the reception tent. They laughed while getting dressed, Emma crabbing about having to do something with her hair so it didn't look like it was mussed from sex.

She found the girls and tried to smile sweetly when they all shot her knowing looks.

"Good, wasn't it?" Abi asked.

Eryn elbowed Abi lightly, "Emma doesn't kiss and tell," she said.

Katherine shook her head, and added, "I hope we all look like that tomorrow morning."

Not expecting such a blatant statement from Katherine, Eryn, Abi, and Emma exchanged looks before laughing.

Braedon made his way to where the groom was standing near the bar.

Chase handed him a beer and said, "I see my wife found you."

Nodding, Braedon took a long pull on his beer and tried not to smile like an idiot.

"Hey," he nodded to Braedon, "we both got lucky."

Looking puzzled, Braedon just smiled.

The DJ announced the throwing of the garter belt and bouquet so people started gathering around the dance floor.

Mitch walked out to the middle of the cleared area and held out his hand for Katherine. She took it and smiled.

The removal of the garter belt was done to cheesy music and had everyone yelling loudly. One of Mitch's cousins won and ran around the floor showing off his prize.

"Now it's the single ladies' turn," the DJ announced. Abi nudged Emma forward.

Emma glared at her friend, "You're single too, you know," she retorted.

Abi grinned, "This engagement ring gives me a buy."

Snarling, Emma went out onto the floor and stood there, feeling like an idiot, as Katherine went to the other end and turned away from the single girls. The music started and the crowd counted with the DJ, "One, two, three!"

Emma stood there, determined to just wait for the humiliating ritual to end.

The little bouquet was thrown and all the single girls were yelling and jumping. Someone bumped into Emma and she glared at the teenage girl. One of the other ladies caught it, thank goodness, and the women were released to go back to their tables.

Emma got back to where Abi and Eryn were sitting with Chase.

"How was it?" Abi asked.

Cocking her head, Emma raised one eyebrow before saying, "What do you think?"

Eryn laughed, "At least you gave it a try," she said.

Abi looked at her friends and knew the teasing was to be expected. They knew what she and Braedon were doing in their room. Not that Emma was embarrassed about it, she'd done her fair share of teasing when each of them were falling in love.

They all sat there, the conversation drifting through different topics. A lot of talk was focused on the double baby shower Eryn's mom was hosting in Hawaii. It was a pretty big affair, from what Eryn and Katherine said.

Emma looked for Braedon but didn't see him. Maybe he was doing something with Gav since he was MIA as well.

"Come on," Gav said as they pulled up in front of a hotel.

When the ladies went out on dance floor, Gav grabbed Braedon and asked if he would help with a little "assignment." Feeling caught up in the festivities, Braedon nodded and followed Abi's fiancé outside.

They were walking through the hotel lobby with a large duffle bag and Braedon was starting to get the picture. They were going to pull some pranks on the bride and groom.

Not that Braedon hadn't participated in some good humored fun over the years, you didn't get through Crash Crew without perfecting the art of the prank, but he thought that short-sheeting the bed or saran-wrapping the toilet seat was kind of juvenile.

They came to a room on the third floor and Gav pulled out the room key.

Once they were inside, Braedon's suspicion was confirmed. The room was most definitely a Bridal Suite.

Braedon was about to object to any possible stunts when Gav opened the bag and pulled out bathrobes.

"Okay," Braedon said, "what's with those?"

Gav smiled, "Eryn and Abi decided that we needed to turn this modest hotel room into a five star hotel for the newlyweds."

Nodding, Braedon opened the bag and took out the chocolates he suspected were the newlyweds' favorite.

Emma was starting to wonder what was going on. She hadn't seen Braedon in almost an hour. She wondered if he was regretting their little intimate session earlier.

Lord knew, she'd regretted some of her actions over the years where men were concerned. But not this one, not with Braedon. It was everything she thought making love should be.

She was blushing and was going to excuse herself to go to the restroom when Eryn's father came over to their table. She'd grown to like General Fredricks since he came around where Eryn and Chase were concerned.

"Hello," Tom Fredricks said when he came up to the table where his daughter and her friends were.

Eryn smiled and said, "Hey, Dad," in return.

Emma figured he was going to ask Eryn to dance but he stepped over beside where Emma was sitting and held his hand out to her.

Surprised, Emma looked up. Mr. Fredricks looked so handsome in his tuxedo. She remembered that he wore his uniform to Eryn's wedding. He was less intimidating in the formal tux he had on now.

Without saying anything, Emma placed her hand into his and they walked out to the dance floor.

Tom took Emma into his embrace and guided her smoothly around the dance floor.

"I wanted to say thank you," he said.

Emma was perplexed and said, "Thank you," she added, "Although I'm not sure what for."

Laughing, Tom spun her around the other couples and said, "For taking your escort away from dancing with my wife."

Trying not to laugh, Emma only nodded.

"You probably think I was being silly," Tom said.

Emma shook her head no, "No, sir, I think you were being a man who appreciated the importance of his wife."

Tom laughed, "You have a knack with making a jealous old codger like me sound almost like a gentleman."

Looking up at General Fredricks, Emma shook her head, "I think I can just read a man in love when I see one."

The song ended and Tom made a production of kissing Emma's hand in thanks.

She walked back to the table where Eryn and Abi were seated.

Eryn looked at her with a side glance and asked, "What was my dad saying to you?"

"He was just saying thanks to me for getting Braedon away from your mom." She chuckled, "It seems that even after being married as long as they have been, he can still get jealous."

Chase sat down next to Eryn and asked, "Who's jealous?"

Play swatting his arm, Eryn answered, "Hopefully you."

Nodding, Chase took a drink of water from Eryn's glass, put it down and responded with, "Every day."

Eryn leaned over and kissed him. It was a kiss that was reassuring and promised more.

Emma watched them and wasn't jealous. She knew that they each found the person they were supposed to be with. There was no way someone could be jealous of that. It was a fate thing.

Braedon and Gav came into the tent and walked over to where the others were seated.

"What did we miss?" Gav asked.

Abi handed him a glass of wine and said, "General Fredricks was thanking Emma for rescuing his marriage."

Puzzled, Gav looked over at Emma, who just shook her head no.

They group sat there for a while, talking about whatever popped into their heads.

Chase asked Braedon about the time he was stationed with Mitch at Quantico, which started a whole new conversation about Crash Crew.

Emma sat back and mostly listened to the conversation. Part of her mind was still upstairs in bed with Braedon and wishing they were still there.

She was so lost in her thoughts that she didn't notice everyone standing up and heading out to the dance floor.

"Hey," Braedon whispered into Emma's ear.

Jumping in surprise, Emma smiled and stood up.

They all danced to the last song of the evening. It was a country song and happened to be one of Emma's favorites.

Braedon danced the two step with Emma and felt like they'd been dancing together for years. She moved so easily in his arms as if they anticipated each other's moves.

The music ended and everyone started making their way toward the house. Braedon went over to where Mitch's parents stood, saying good night to guests. He waited patiently for Aly Frinnel to acknowledge him.

"Braedon," she said, while leaning over to kiss his cheek, "we hope you had a good time."

Braedon smiled and nodded while saying, "Yes, ma'am." He nodded to Matt Frinnel before asking, "Is there something I can help you with?"

Aly already had a high opinion of Emma's escort. The offer just lifted him into an even higher level. She smiled brightly.

"No, I think the catering company is taking care of clean up, but thank you so much for offering." She patted his hand.

He nodded once again and continued on toward the house.

Not seeing Emma, Braedon made his way upstairs. He opened the door to their room and smiled at the sound of the shower coming from the bathroom.

Emma saw Braedon make a detour toward Mitch's parents so she took the opportunity to run upstairs and get into the shower. They'd made love, yes, but the other stuff like using the bathroom and showering was still private.

She'd piled her hair up on her head and just washed her body. Her skin was sensitive in spots, she assumed from their lovemaking. It reminded her that she wasn't a nun after all.

She was stepping out of the tub when she saw Braedon appear at the doorway of the bathroom. Smiling, she grabbed a towel and wrapped it around her body.

"I've already seen what's under there," Braedon teased her.

Emma looked at him, eyes slit, "And if you're not nice to me, you'll never see it again."

'Point made,' Braedon thought. He smiled and left the doorway to get his pajamas.

Making quick work of her nighttime ritual, Emma put cream on her face and elbows. She had a separate lotion for her legs and arms to prevent dry skin. Over the years, men commented on how soft her skin was. If they only knew how much time it took to keep it that way.

She came out of the bathroom to see Braedon sitting in the chair across the room. He was on the phone and talking quietly.

Not wanting to eavesdrop, she went back into the bathroom and got her brush out of the toiletry bag to begin working through the knots her wedding updo created.

Ten minutes later, she was still trying to detangle it when she saw Braedon's reflection in the mirror.

He smiled and offered, "I can help you with that, you know."

Chapter 17

Sunday morning, Emma woke up to a noise she couldn't decipher. She opened one eye to look around. She was facing the window of the bedroom so her first view of the day was a large white tent being lowered. They must be cleaning up from the wedding.

She opened the other eye and rolled over. The smile she had on disappeared when she found that Braedon was not beside her.

The night before was sweet; she smiled and snuggled deeper into bed while thinking about it.

Braedon had brushed her long hair until it was smooth. They had sat on the bed, her in front of him, as he slowly worked through the snarls. She probably would've complained more but feeling his legs surrounding hers caused her to focus more on her body's awareness of him.

After he finished, he put the brush down on the nightstand and ran his fingers through her hair.

Emma was in some sort of trance as his fingers moved over her scalp and down her back.

After a few minutes, she turned around and stared at him until he kissed her.

They made love one more time before drifting off to sleep, wrapped up in one another's arms.

Emma sighed and decided that it was time to get up. Lovely dream or memories couldn't put off the day.

She got up and went into the bathroom to shower.

Braedon brought a tray upstairs in the hopes of waking Emma up. He quietly opened the door and frowned when he saw she wasn't in bed. The shower was on so put the tray down on a nearby table and waited for her come out.

Emma washed her hair to get out the mousse and hairspray the hairdresser put in the day before. She was humming as she walked out of the bathroom. Surprise washed across her features when she found Braedon in the room.

"Good morning," she said, feeling slightly self-conscious in only a towel.

Braedon couldn't think about anything else except Emma. She was just so damn beautiful!

He stood up and walked to her.

Wrapping his hands around her shoulders, he said, "Good morning to you."

Emma smiled. There was something funny going on inside of her and she couldn't pinpoint it.

Braedon turned and motioned to the tray before asking, "Are you hungry?"

Not wanting to sound too perverted, Emma shrugged and walked over to the overstuffed chair.

She smelled the coffee and lifted the cup to her lips. She liked her coffee with one cream and one sugar and wondered how he figured that out.

"It's perfect," she said as she lifted the cup in a kind of toast.

He sat down on the edge of the bed and absently straightened the comforter around him before saying, "Eryn gave me specific instructions."

Emma didn't doubt it for one moment. Eryn probably knew everything about her and then some.

Nibbling on some toast, Emma motioned toward the window, "I see they're taking it all down."

Braedon nodded yes and just stared at her.

"What's on the docket for today?" Emma asked, trying to stave off any awkwardness for the "morning after."

Standing up, Braedon walked to where she sat and crouched down. He took her hand in his.

Smiling, he said, "We're pretty much left to our own devices today from what I've heard."

"What are the others doing?" Emma asked as she neatly stacked the dishes he brought in.

Looking at Emma, Braedon could see this was tough for her. He wanted to say he could understand but he couldn't. Things were different and it was clear to him that they were now lovers and a couple.

He stood and pulled her up so she was standing in front of him.

Brushing hair from her face, he said, "It doesn't have to be weird, you know."

Half smiling and half frowning, Emma moved around him and went into the bathroom.

She was thankful for the distraction of doing her hair and makeup. It gave her a few minutes to get her bearings. He messed with her insides when he was anywhere near her and that bugged the hell out of her.

Fifteen minutes later, Emma emerged from the bathroom and felt much better. She had on faded jeans that covered her knee high boots. Her shirt was long sleeved, light pink, and silk so it literally skimmed across her skin. The combination of casual with elegant made her feel confident. The smile she put on for Braedon disappeared when she came back out and saw an empty room.

Braedon took the tray downstairs with the intention of giving Emma some time alone and himself some time to get his impulses under control.

Just looking at her took him back to the night before and how she looked as they made love. He didn't just see her beautiful physical qualities but he knew he struck a chord inside of her. And if there was one thing Braedon learned about her in the short time they'd known one another, it was that she wouldn't like being read that easily.

Once he walked into the kitchen, he saw Mrs. Frinnel at the stove cooking. Eryn and Chase were at the table with Abi and Gav. They all looked at him when he went to the sink and put the dishes inside it.

"Good morning," Gav said in a bright voice.

Turning around, Braedon replied, "Good morning."

Aly Frinnel walked a pan of eggs over to the table and started dishing them onto plates.

She winked at Abi and said, "I can tell you that he came down and got that tray to take upstairs to Miss Emma."

"Oh," Eryn said. "How is Miss Emma this morning, Braedon?" she asked slowly.

Putting the tray back into a nearby cupboard, Braedon waited to answer. He was going to say something when Emma beat him to it.

"I'm just fine, Mrs. Johnson. How are you doing?" Emma asked from the kitchen doorway.

All eyes turned to her and Emma felt like a science experiment or something.

She tried to be nonchalant and walked over to where Braedon was standing. Without saying anything, she gave him a kiss on the lips then stood next to him with her arm around his waist.

Eryn looked at Abi and just smiled.

Braedon knew something was going on between Emma and her friends but didn't know what it meant.

Emma looked at her friends. "Are we going out or what?" she asked sarcastically.

No one answered. They all turned around and dug into their breakfasts. Of course, every one of them was smiling.

Braedon didn't know what he missed but it was something.

"Are you hungry?" Emma asked him as she turned to face him.

He shook his head no and answered, "I ate earlier when Mrs. Frinnel was making up your tray."

"Aly," Mrs. Frinnel piped in.

Smiling, Braedon nodded and looked over at Mitch's mom.

Emma liked his smile. It was warm and welcoming. Much like the man himself, she supposed.

"Let's go for a walk," Emma whispered.

She walked over to a closet off the kitchen and grabbed coats for them. Tossing one to Braedon, Emma slipped the other one on.

Braedon nodded and allowed her to lead the way out the back door.

As soon as she and Braedon were outside, she heard the voices start up in the kitchen. Smiling to herself, she knew the girls were going to explain to the guys what happened.

Braedon put his hand on Emma's back as they started to walk. It was pretty lovely for being October in the northeast. No snow was on the ground but the wind did have a bit of a bite to it.

All the remnants of the tent were packed up and being hauled off so they walked in the opposite direction to avoid getting in the crew's way.

Braedon looked around as they walked and found that he could understand why the Frinnel's loved this place. Even at this time of year, with the trees almost bare, it was beautiful. In the distance he could see rows of evergreen trees that stood regally on a rise.

"Are you okay?" Emma asked.

She didn't care for how insecure she sounded. Like she'd never slept with someone before; she knew the drill of the morning after. Not well, but she did.

Braedon stopped and turned so they were facing one another. He brought his hands up so they were cupping her face.

Without answering her question, Braedon brought his lips downward so they met with hers. He kissed her softly.

When he finished, he brought his forehead to hers before saying, "That's what I'm thinking."

Emma felt so strange. He wasn't at all what she expected. It was nice but made her very uneasy. She couldn't answer him, so she only nodded.

They continued walking for a while until Mitch's niece Allison ran out to find them. She explained that the others were leaving and Emma and Braedon would be left behind if they didn't get a move on.

"Nice," Emma said dryly when the little girl ran back to the house.

Braedon chuckled, "They're your friends."

"And I wouldn't trade them for the world," Emma said seriously.

He nodded and took her hand in his so they could start back to the house.

Once everyone was together, the group loaded up into vehicles and went into town.

No one had any specific plans so they parked and started walking with no destination. Mitch and Katherine were wrapped up in one another and none of the other couples minded one bit. They deserved all the happiness they could find.

Braedon walked with his hand around Emma's and laughed at something Gav said.

Emma took the time to just listen. She wanted to know how Braedon acted around her friends. They were the most important people in her life besides her family and their opinion meant a lot to her.

The group darted in and out of some stores and joked about whatever came to mind. It was easy and everyone was in good spirits which helped a lot.

"So, Braedon," Katherine said as they were leaving an antique store, "how was it working with my husband?"

Braedon smiled, "He was very professional, ma'am."

Chase chimed in and asked, "Okay how much money did he give you to say that crap?"

Everyone laughed and kept going.

Not being one to lie, Braedon answered, "No money exchanged hands, but he saved me from a nasty run in with a Staff Sgt. who was way too big for his britches."

Mitch laughed, "Oh yeah, that one who thought you weren't supposed to boss him around."

Nodding, Braedon smiled and squeezed Emma's hand.

The group started talking about different run-ins they'd had over their careers and everyone laughed and tried to one up the others'.

It was late afternoon when they returned to Mitch's parents' place. There were cars in the driveway so they ended up parking on the roadside next to it.

Mitch's mother was waiting on the porch with hands on her hips.

She pointed to Mitch and Katherine and asked, "Did you two forget that you had a gift opening today?"

Mitch climbed the steps with his bride and leaned over to kiss his mother on the cheek before saying, "We didn't forget, Mom."

Aly smiled and shooed them all inside.

Katherine's parents were there, along with Eryn's, and they were chatting with one of Mitch's aunts when the group came in.

Aly herded the bride and groom into the living room to begin opening up presents.

Emma stood in the doorway next to Braedon and watched them with a smile on her face.

Being the Matron of Honor, Eryn sat next to Katherine and dutifully took down the gifts and who sent them. Emma laughed at how serious Eryn looked. She remembered, just six months earlier, helping Eryn with the same task.

"My turn to ask what you're thinking about," Braedon whispered into Emma's ear.

Smiling at him, Emma said, "How glad I am to not have to worry about all of this." She motioned to the gifts and crowd.

Not knowing exactly how to take the comment, Braedon just nodded and went back to watching the festivities.

After all the gifts were opened and logged, the group went into the kitchen where Aly Frinnel put out a buffet.

Braedon went over to Mitch's mother and asked, "Is there anything I can help you with, Aly?" He remembered to call her by her first name.

Aly smiled and gave him a kiss on the cheek, "You're a sweet man, Braedon, but we've got it all set."

He nodded and added, "I just know my momma would skin me if I didn't pitch in to earn my keep."

'Oh,' Aly thought, 'no wonder Emma is so out of sorts, he's a charmer like no other.'

She brushed the lipstick residue she left on his cheek off and said, "Your momma would be proud, Braedon."

He nodded and murmured, "Thank you, ma'am."

Aly stood where she was and watched Braedon walk back over to where Emma, Abi, Eryn, and Katherine stood talking.

She thought that if Emma wasn't careful, he was going to catch her.

The group talked all through the dinner and well into the evening. Mitch's various family members would join them on and off but mainly let the friends reminisce and talk about the upcoming baby showers and wedding.

Braedon was torn. On one level, he knew he was a part of the group. But on another level, he couldn't help but catch the words Emma used. She only said, "I" when she talked about the plans.

He wasn't sure if it was on purpose or a slip but, either way, it didn't feel too good.

They were winding down mid-evening, when Eryn spoke to Braedon saying, "I hope you are into baby showers, Braedon."

He smiled and looked to Emma for an answer. She acted like she didn't hear it so he let it go.

As everyone went up to their rooms, Emma thought about what was said. The others already included Braedon. It's what she wanted originally but now she wasn't really sure.

Chapter 18

Braedon woke up Monday morning and felt a kind of dread sneak up his spine. The night before didn't go as he planned it and he didn't know what happened exactly.

Sitting up in bed, he went over the scene in his mind once again.

He and Emma came upstairs and got into their room with no problems. She told him he could use the bathroom first so he got ready for bed. When he came out, he looked at her and thought maybe she'd been crying.

His first mistake was to ask her about it. He didn't think he'd ever seen a woman's anger flare up that fast in his life. She accused him of being too nice to her and her friends and was rambling on.

He only stood there and took it because he didn't know how to respond and had a sneaking suspicion that she was looking for any bit of ammunition to use.

She stomped to the bathroom after realizing she couldn't rile him up into a fight. He went to bed and turned off the light so she wouldn't see him look worried.

They slept without touching and Braedon wondered if she felt as bad as he did.

Looking over, he saw Emma laying there with her eyes open, watching him.

"Good morning," he said softly.

Tears sprang to Emma's eyes immediately and that really pissed her off.

She didn't like crying and was always told it was a sign of weakness. If she was going to cry then she'd better have a really good reason to do it.

Responding to Braedon, she whispered, "Good morning."

He sat there, a grin on his face, looking at her.

She managed to hide her tears with wiping her face before sitting up. She knew she should say she was sorry for her behavior but it was difficult.

Braedon thought she looked beautiful with her hair covering her shoulders and her cheeks rosy from sleep.

"I guess," Emma started, "we should get going."

Nodding, Braedon wondered if she would open up.

An hour later, they were downstairs, bags in tow, and eating some breakfast before heading to the airport.

There was only them and Mitch's parents so the noise level was a lot less than the last few days.

Mitch and Katherine were flying out later in the day to the Caribbean for their honeymoon. Then they would be starting their new life in Quantico, Virginia, where Mitch was stationed.

The guys got up right after breakfast and went out to load up the luggage, leaving the girls inside.

"I don't like this part," Abi said as she tried to hold back emotions.

Emma felt the same way but never let on. "Oh, it's only a month or so until the baby shower so hold on to your horses there."

Abi laughed and nodded.

Eryn sighed, and started, "I forgot to tell you," she rushed, "that the mothers are changing the baby shower to Virginia instead of Hawaii. It was easier for them."

Katherine and Abi nodded but Emma felt a little let down. She liked Virginia just fine but really loved Hawaii. What use was it to have friends there if you couldn't see them?

Eryn explained that Victoria and Beverly were both hosting the baby shower and it was going to be a large one. So large, in fact, that they were reserving a ballroom at a swanky hotel.

"Geez," Emma said dryly, "do these kids actually care where it's held?"

Abi laughed and Eryn tipped her head to glare at her friend.

Katherine said, "No, but if this is what our mothers want to do, we won't stop them."

Emma mumbled, "I suppose," and let it drop.

They moved on to Abi's wedding preparations and Emma started to tune out. Her thoughts were focused on a certain Marine whose smile made her stomach flip and threatened to turn her world upside down if she let him.

Of course, she wouldn't do that so this train of thought was moot.

Braedon walked into the kitchen and stopped. He saw Eryn, Abi, and Katherine discussing wedding plans and Emma sitting there, lost in thought. Her face was set in a frown and he was thinking it probably had something to do with him. Egotistical? Maybe.

Feeling Braedon's hands on her shoulders, Emma's frown turned into a smile as she looked up.

He was really very handsome in a chiseled way. She imagined a lot of women probably discarded him with the silent thing he had going on. She sort of did, at first. But once you got underneath that protective façade, he was charming and funny.

'Quit!' she yelled to herself. 'He's just a man, nothing more.'

Braedon smiled and asked, "Are you ready?"

Emma nodded and wondered if there was some additional meaning in the question.

They filed outside and gave Mitch's parents hugs and words of thanks.

Aly Frinnel shook Braedon's hand and commented, "You've got a tough cookie there," as she nodded to Emma.

Braedon agreed and smiled before saying, "Yes, ma'am, I think I do."

"It's been my experience," Aly said, "that the hardest ones are worth the effort."

Not knowing how to respond to her, Braedon just kept smiling. He wasn't sure if it was an observation or advice she was giving him.

A few minutes later, the six of them were on their way up to Philadelphia. Mitch and Katherine were going up later since their flight wasn't until the evening.

It was decided that Abi would ride with Gav in his car while the others loaded up in the van. The girls were once again in the backseat and talking about whatever.

Chase was looking over at Braedon periodically and wanted to ask him a few questions but wasn't sure where to start. He didn't have to worry, Braedon spoke first.

"You're worried," Braedon said lowly.

Nodding, Chase smiled at the man's ability to pick up on things.

Braedon nodded, "I won't hurt her if I can avoid it," he said seriously.

Chase knew he didn't have a right to ask anything of Braedon. He wasn't Emma's father but he sure felt like her big brother and, as such, he felt he needed to protect her.

Looking in the rearview to make sure the girls were still talking, he nodded and looked over before saying, "You understand that I have to ask though, right?"

Braedon nodded again, "I understand. I hope my sister has someone to look out for her like you and Mitch look out for Emma."

"Oh, Gav wanted to hire a private eye to check you out but Mitch vouched for you," Chase said softly.

Chase kept an eye on the girls to make sure they weren't listening to the conversation in the front seat. Emma would blow a gasket if she found out her "brothers" were doing stuff like that.

Feeling relieved that he knew Mitch, Braedon tried not to laugh at the guys' antics. He realized this was serious to them but he meant what he said about not hurting Emma. That was the last thing he wanted to do.

After a few minutes, curiosity got to Braedon and he asked, "What did Mitch say exactly?"

Now it was Chase's turn to hold back a laugh. He knew it was a gamble to reveal some of the stuff Gav, Mitch, and he were discussing.

"Well, he said you were a good guy, which wasn't a surprise," Chase started. "Then he said he'd trust you with his life and that was good enough for us."

Braedon made a mental note to thank Mitch. They'd only worked together for about a year before Braedon got orders to California but it was nice to know he had made that good of an impression on Mitch during that time. He thought highly of Mitch as well and would probably say the same of him.

The drive to the airport was easy since their flight was leaving late morning and the traffic was light.

Chase and Braedon got out the luggage as Eryn turned the paperwork into the rental company.

Abi and Gav were parking in the short term parking since Gav was driving his own car back to New York after Abi was settled in for her flight.

"Ready?" Eryn asked when they were all waiting to get on the shuttle to the airport.

Emma nodded, but didn't smile.

Cocking her head, Eryn gave the "spill it" look to her friend.

Knowing Eryn was like a dog with a bone when it came to weaseling out information, Emma decided it was better to just be forthcoming.

She sighed and said, "He confuses me."

Eryn nodded, "Oh I'm sure," she shook her head at the look Emma shot her, "And I'm only saying that some men just do that to us."

"Yeah, well," Emma said and took a peek to see where the guys were before asking, "and who was the last guy to do that to you?"

Laughing, Eryn thought her friend was being silly considering how smart Emma was in almost every facet of her life.

Pointing to Chase, Eryn answered, "He's right there."

Emma knew she'd walked into that one and smiled as she dropped her head.

They hugged hard, knowing that being apart would make it harder.

The men joined them and everyone piled into the shuttle.

Braedon sat next to Emma on the shuttle and knew she was thinking about something very hard. He hoped it was him but suspected that he was only a small part of what occupied Ms. Emma Cantrell's mind.

The shuttle arrived at the airport and dropped them off. Gav and Abi were standing just inside and were wrapped up in one another. Emma and Eryn exchanged a look and didn't say anything.

"Well," Emma turned to Chase, "you take care of my girl there or I'll come to Hawaii and kick your ass."

She leaned forward and gave him a quick hug and kiss.

Chase tried to look scared, "Okay, just for you."

Nodding, Emma turned to see Eryn talking to Braedon. Whatever she said made him give her a look of surprise. That didn't sit well with Emma at all.

Everyone grabbed their bags and went inside to say goodbye to Abi and Gav before splitting up and heading out to their respective gates.

Braedon shook Gav's hand and said, "It was very nice to meet you."

Gav responded with, "You too, man, I wish you luck."

That's what Eryn said to him too. He was wondering if everyone knew something he didn't.

Goodbyes were said, a few tears were shed, and everyone split up.

Braedon and Emma walked to their airline counter to get their luggage checked.

They were on the way to their gate before she spoke.

"Thanks again for coming with me," Emma said, almost shyly, to him.

Braedon took her carry on from her and tossed it onto the seat they were standing next to before taking her into his arms and kissing her hard.

The only thing Emma could think was, 'He always takes me by surprise.'

Thinking that she would put up more guards emotionally, Braedon wanted to get into her mind as much as possible.

He kissed her thoroughly and set her back away from him.

"Now," Braedon said, "That was a thank you."

Looking up at him and smiling, Emma said, "I guess so."

They sat down and waited for their flight in silence, each of them thinking about what happened over the weekend.

Chapter 19

Almost a week later, Emma was on the phone talking with Eryn when the question she knew would pop up, did.

"How's Braedon?" Eryn asked.

They'd been talking for close to an hour and Emma never mentioned him. Eryn thought that was kind of odd so she brought him up herself.

Emma sighed and answered in a clipped tone, "I don't know, I'm not his keeper."

Shaking her head in exasperation, Eryn tried to remain calm. Being almost six months pregnant, she had a hard time keeping her emotions in balance.

"Well, you've certainly seen him since the trip, right?" Eryn asked.

Sitting there on her patio, Emma didn't want to answer the question.

Sighing, Eryn asked, "You haven't talked to him, have you?"

Murmuring, Emma said, "No."

"Em," Eryn whined, but didn't get any farther since Emma cut her off.

She snapped, "Don't!" to Eryn and said, "The flight was fine and he dropped me off here and we just haven't coordinated our schedules."

"Emma, it's not like you both are so busy that you can't get together," Eryn said in a clipped tone.

Not wanting the lecture, Emma just didn't answer.

They hung up a few minutes later and Emma knew her friend was upset. Hell, she was upset herself. She didn't tell Braedon not to call her or see her. He'd dropped her off at her place and brought her bag up to the door. Yes, she'd admit that she hadn't invited him inside. Maybe it was stupid on her part but, at the time, she was tired and needed some distance.

She assumed he would call her within a day or two but there was only total phone silence. Now it was Saturday and she was about to go crazy from frustration.

Going inside, she tossed her phone onto the counter and got a bottled water from the refrigerator.

The cool liquid did nothing to wash away the lump in her throat. It had been there since the Monday before and couldn't be eased.

Looking at the clock, Emma realized it was barely six in the evening and she'd go nuts if she had to stay at home for one more night. Grabbing her phone, she went upstairs.

An hour later, she was on her way north on the 15 Freeway.

She wouldn't admit that she was going to Bullz in the hopes of seeing Braedon. She just liked the place and wanted to get out. His brother, Jason, did say that she was welcome any time.

Tonight she was dressed more appropriately in form-fitting jeans, a tank with sequins on it, and some hopelessly expensive cowboy boots.

After finding a parking space, Emma checked her reflection in the mirror and, feeling satisfied, got out of the car to head inside.

The place was loud and boisterous and Emma immediately felt better. She needed a distraction.

Not five feet inside the door, she was stopped by a man in a black cowboy hat.

"Want to dance, pretty lady?" he asked.

Emma thought he was probably well on his way to intoxication and didn't want to touch that problem with a ten-foot pole.

She smiled and said, "I'm sorry, sweetie, but my boyfriend is right over there." Walking around him, she added, "But thank you so much for the offer."

The man shrugged and went on his way so Emma turned to go toward the bar. She stood there for a few minutes before a pretty woman bartender came over to her.

"What can I get you?" the woman asked brightly.

Emma read her nametag that said "Kathy."

Leaning forward so she wouldn't have to yell, Emma asked, "How about a whiskey?"

Kathy nodded and left. When she came back, she put the shot on the bar and poured it with a flourish.

Emma took the glass and downed it quickly. She slammed the empty glass on the bar and nodded for another.

"Well," Kathy said, "a woman who slams a fine whiskey like that probably has man trouble."

Rolling her eyes, Emma was about to nod when Jason appeared right beside Kathy, a smile on his face.

Jason saw the pretty Emma as soon as she entered. It was hard for any man not to notice her as she had looks that should grace the covers of magazines. Of course, that woman also had her brother tied up in knots and that, he found, was not a good thing.

Braedon dropped off his car the Monday before and looked like he had the world on his shoulders. It had been a good, long while since Braedon looked like that.

"Well, well," Jason said to Emma, snapping out of his thoughts.

She lifted the shot glass in a salute and downed it quickly. Knowing that was enough for now, she shook her head no when Kathy raised the bottle to pour another.

Looking at Jason, she asked, "Kathy, would you mind getting me a water?"

'Oh this one, she knows what she does to men,' Jason thought to himself.

Jason leaned on the bar and asked, "So what brings you round these parts, pretty lady?"

The whiskey was already starting its hypnotic spell on her brain. Of course, that made her tongue loose.

She shot back, "A night of not wanting to be alone."

Her response surprised Jason. Surely Braedon wouldn't refuse a woman he was dating. That just didn't sound like him. Of course, it really was none of his business what Braedon did or didn't do.

He was about to comment about Braedon when a man came up to where Emma was standing and asked her to dance.

With two whiskey shots in her, Emma was loosened up and nodded before they made their way to the dance floor.

Leaving the bar area, Jason motioned to Kathy that he would be right back and headed to his office. It was only feet off the main bar floor and that made it easier for him to go out if there were any issues.

He went into his office and picked up his cell phone. Pushing the number for Braedon he waited impatiently for his brother to answer.

"Hey Jas," Braedon said.

Anger flashed through Jason, and he snapped, "You'd better get up here. Now."

The man that asked Emma to dance was so nice. She thought he said his name was Doug but she wasn't sure. The shots took effect quickly and she was buzzed big time.

They circled the floor to keep up with the quick beat of the music and Emma wanted to throw her hair back and yell with the freedom she was feeling.

She didn't need one man, she needed to have fun and let loose, and that was all!

Doug, or whatever his name was, just kept up the pace until the song ended.

She was smiling at him and about to say something when she caught a glimpse of the man now standing behind him.

Braedon made it up to his brother's bar in less than a half hour. He didn't know what the emergency was but he told Jason he'd come so he did.

Now he was here and didn't see Jason right away. Making eye contact with the main bartender, Kathy, Braedon nodded.

She pointed to the dance floor so Braedon looked over. He didn't see Jason so he was going to turn toward the office area when his gaze caught sight of Emma.

At first, he just stood there and watched her. Seeing her decked out in jeans and that shirt, his mouth went dry.

She looked like she was born on a farm, country girl from head to toe. It amazed him how she could transform herself to fit into any situation.

The guy she was dancing with was pretty handsy and that made Braedon's shackles go up.

He made his way toward them and was about to cut in when they separated because the music stopped.

"Braedon," Emma whispered.

He looked……hot! He had on a plaid, form fitting shirt with the sleeves rolled up, and a pair of jeans that made his legs look long and lean. Of course, the look in his eyes was like shooting daggers so she knew a fight was coming.

The man she was dancing with turned to see Braedon and could see the look of "mine" written on Braedon's face. He excused himself, not wanting to get into a fight tonight.

Braedon watched the other man leave and was about to say something when a slow song started. Instead, he just walked up and took Emma into his arms.

"What are you doing?" he asked in a tight voice.

Emma recognized that he was holding his temper, she did the same thing. Personally, she thought he didn't have anything to be angry about.

Stiffening in his embrace, she snapped, "I'm out having a good time."

He didn't doubt it. If Emma was determined, then she'd do something.

They moved around the dance floor easily. Emma felt safe in his arms and resented him for it. She didn't want to "like" being with him. When the song ended, Emma dropped her arms and left him standing there.

He followed her to the bar where she ordered another shot from Kathy. He nodded when the bartender looked to him. She knew he'd never let Emma drive after drinking.

Emma thanked Kathy and lifted the glass to her lips. The whiskey burned a little as it went down her throat, but the numbing feeling it gave her was worth it. After setting the shot glass down on the bar she turned around to face Braedon.

"So what are you doing here?" Emma asked him.

Braedon stepped forward and put one arm against the bar. He'd like to say it was to keep her from moving but it was really so he wouldn't touch her. Every part of him wanted to pick her up and take her to his place so he could make love to her all night.

He shrugged and answered, "I was just out and thought I'd stop by. I didn't expect to see you."

'Really?' Emma thought.

"Do you think I don't go out and know how to have a good time, Braedon?" she asked loudly.

He knew the alcohol was making her bold and he really didn't care, as long as he got her home.

Emma started to rant, "I mean, there are actually men here who want to be with me."

The verbal jab hurt, he admitted it to himself, but not to her. He didn't answer.

Jason walked up to them just then. Emma smiled brightly and leaned on him.

She played with the collar of Jason's shirt and asked, "How 'bout a dance, cowboy?"

Jason laughed and nodded.

Braedon watched as Jason led her to the dance floor; anger pulsed through him the whole time. Frustrated, he turned around to face the bar and his eyes found Kathy's looking the same way.

Over the last couple of years he and Kathy went out a few times, mostly as friends. Braedon liked her well enough but there was something that held him off. It was her obvious feelings for his brother and he recognized them now as she watched Jason and Emma on the dance floor.

He could honestly say he knew exactly how she felt.

Ordering a soda, Braedon waited until Jason brought Emma back a few minutes later.

She ordered yet another shot and Jason motioned to Kathy that it was her last one for the night.

The bartender nodded subtly and smiled at Emma as she poured.

After that shot, Emma was wobbly so she sat on the bar stool and looked at Braedon. He was standing there and saying absolutely nothing...and that drove her nuts!

"What's going on, Braedon?" Emma finally asked when she couldn't take it anymore.

Looking at Emma, Braedon measured his words before speaking.

He put his hand on hers and said, "I'm making sure you get home alright."

Emma's head snapped around and she glared at Jason, who was now standing beside Kathy behind the bar.

Jason put up his hands in mock surrender while Kathy suddenly became very busy with customers at the other end of the bar.

Seeing that she had no one to blame but herself, Emma dropped her head and tried not to cry.

"Let's get you home," Braedon said into her ear and helped her off the stool.

Nodding, because there was no other logical answer, Emma got up. She was pissed that she had to lean on him to walk.

They managed to get out to his car and he helped her get inside.

Sitting quietly, Emma allowed him to handle her. It wasn't an easy thing for her to do as she'd never done it before.

Getting into the driver's seat, Braedon started up the car and pulled out of the spot.

He made quick work of getting onto the freeway and heading south toward Emma's place.

Emma didn't say anything during the drive home. She kept teetering between being mad and being ashamed that she'd gotten drunk.

Half an hour later, Braedon pulled into the driveway of her place. He turned off the car and sat there, studying her. Sometime during the ride, she'd fallen asleep. Watching her was like going to a museum and seeing an exquisite piece of art.

Emma stirred when she no longer heard the hum of the engine. Looking over, she met Braedon's eyes. He looked intense and it made her self-conscious.

"We're home?" she asked.

Braedon nodded, "Yes, wait there and I'll come around to help you."

Emma did as he said and waited for him to come around.

He helped her stand and gauged whether or not she was steady before allowing her to walk toward the front door.

They were at the stoop when Emma's phone started ringing. She groped her pockets and fumbled as she pulled it out. Looking at the screen, she saw it was Abi and decided to ignore it. She just wasn't in the mood for a pep talk or lecture right now.

Braedon waited for her to open the door and step inside before he said, "Get some sleep, I'll come by tomorrow to help you get your car."

Realizing that she'd forgotten about her car all together, Emma groaned out, "Yeah, sure, I'll see you then."

He started walking away and Emma felt even more lost than she did earlier.

Chapter 20

Sunday morning came early and Emma woke up feeling awful!

Looking in the bathroom mirror, she cringed at the sight of herself. She neglected to take off her make up from the night before so her face was streaked with it. Her hair looked like a rugby match was played in it. A shower and coffee were what she needed……the sooner the better.

After showering and scrubbing her face clean, she wrapped herself in a bathrobe and went downstairs to start the coffee.

Standing there, she was waiting for the machine to finish when there was a knock on the door.

Thinking it was Braedon, she did a quick check of herself in the hall mirror and went to open the front door.

It wasn't Braedon at the door, but Dave.

"Good morning," Dave said smiling.

Stepping back so he could come in, she answered, "Good morning."

She shut the door and felt really weird standing there in her robe talking to Dave.

"I'll just run up and change quickly," she said as she moved around him, "you help yourself to coffee and I'll be right down."

Dave nodded and headed to the kitchen.

Emma was upstairs and heard a loud noise from the kitchen. She ran to the stairs and yelled down, "Are you okay?"

Coming into the hallway, Dave was using a towel to try and wipe the coffee off of his now drenched shirt, "The coffee maker and I had an accident," he said.

Emma tried to cover her mouth with her hand so he wouldn't see her laugh.

"Uh," she said, "throw the shirt in the washer and I'll get you a t-shirt to wear."

Dave nodded and disappeared around the corner while Emma went back into her room to finish getting dressed.

The washer was going and Dave was cleaning up the mess in the kitchen when the doorbell rang. He didn't hear Emma upstairs so he went to answer it. Opening the door, he came face to face with Braedon.

"Hey," Dave said, a smile on his face.

Braedon expected to see Emma so he was smiling. But instead he was greeted with a shirtless Dave. What the hell?

At that moment, Emma came downstairs and said, "I got you a shirt, now try to keep this one on."

Her words and smile faded as she realized that Dave was at the front door with no shirt on and facing an angry looking Braedon. She was still in her bathrobe which didn't help one bit if Braedon's look gave any indication.

His stomach was in his feet and Braedon didn't even remember what he said to either of them. He only turned around and went to get into his car and drive home.

Emma knew what he thought, she would've probably thought the same thing if she walked into this.

Dave looked at her and asked, "Did we just screw up?"

Not bothering to answer, Emma only nodded and tried not to cry.

Monday morning, Braedon was on his way to work when his phone went off. It was Emma, again.

Since the previous morning, she had called him a dozen times. She left messages saying that he misunderstood the situation and asked him to call her.

Every part of him wanted to call her but he thought it might be a losing battle on his part. After all, he wasn't even in her league in most areas.

He'd heard through Jason that her car had been picked up and he was glad about that at least. Although seeing her and Dave look like they did, made his blood boil. He spent the previous day catching up on errands and trying not to drive over there and give her a piece of his mind.

She didn't leave a message and the phone was quiet once again.

Emma went to work on Monday with sour look and an even worse attitude. Not the best way to start her week, but it was how she felt.

This morning she was pissed…..that Braedon wouldn't even call her back to hear her explanation about what happened. She had to ask Dave to run her up to the bar to pick up her car and half expected to see Braedon's car there.

The rest of the day was spent pouting about how Braedon was being so unreasonable.

This morning, she was driving in and happened to stop at an intersection to wait for a red light. Sitting there, she was thinking about what she would say to him, how she would kick his ass with her words, when she saw his car go through the intersection from the opposite way.

Her light turned green and she ended up being right behind him on the road that led to the flight line.

How she'd never noticed his car before now, was amazing. They worked in buildings that were literally right next to one another but never so much as crossed paths, at least that she noticed.

She watched him pull into a spot across from Crash Crew and kept going to her assigned spot across from the Airfield Operations building.

After parking, she grabbed her bag and got out of her car. She was walking across the street when she noticed him. He was standing just outside the Crash Crew door watching her.

She had two choices here. She could either acknowledge him and hope that they could talk or she could keep walking as if she hadn't noticed him.

Deciding that she'd never backed down from a fight before, she changed direction and headed toward his building.

Braedon saw her as soon as his car passed hers on base. He watched her pass him when he parked and took the time to watch her as she got out of her car and started walking. He should've known she'd notice him staring.

"Good morning," Emma said tentatively as she neared him.

Nodding, Braedon answered, "Good morning, Master Guns."

'So this was how it is?' Emma commented to herself.

Standing up straighter, Emma decided no time like now to open up the can of worms that was this weekend.

"I realize that you deserve an explanation," she started but quickly stopped when she saw his face morph into a grim line.

Braedon didn't expect her to dive into what happened and, personally, he didn't want to hear it. Dave never hid how he felt about her and she responded. The fact that knowing she was with Dave after she was with him rubbed him raw.

He stood straight and answered, "No explanations necessary, Master Guns, I think I understand."

Without waiting for her to respond, Braedon nodded to her, then turned and went into the Crash Crew building.

Seething from his brush off, Emma stood there for a minute or two and tried to get her temper in check before going into the Airfield Operations building. She just kept repeating "stubborn ass," to herself for the morning.

At lunch time, Braedon made his way over to the food court near the main Exchange on the base. He offered to pick up food for his OIC and a few of the others just so he had an excuse to get out for a little bit.

He remembered how he shut Emma down this morning and was ashamed of his behavior. He was raised by a mother who pounded manners into him and his siblings and here he was, being about as rude as can be.

As if his thinking about her manifested reality, Emma came into his line of sight while he was waiting for his order to be made.

Emma went to the food court for lunch and didn't see Braedon until she was in line to order. He looked upset and she was glad. He deserved to feel awful for the way he treated her.

Swallowing his pride and a healthy dose of guilty, Braedon walked over to where Emma was in line.

"Hello, Master Gunnery Sgt.," he said quietly.

Watching him, Emma was brought to tears. They had spent a weekend together and she thought maybe they had something but then he never even called her! How could someone do that if they really cared about you? 'Because he doesn't care!' she yelled at herself.

Deciding that food wasn't appealing anymore, Emma tried to smile weakly and walked away. She didn't bother to look back and see Braedon standing there, watching her.

Later that night, Emma's phone rang. Picking it up, she saw it was Abi again. She thought, 'Might as well get it over with,' and hit the accept button.

"What?" she asked in a bright voice.

To anyone else who didn't know Emma well, they would've thought that she was being sarcastic. But Abi knew her too well and could see through the act.

Smiling, Abi said, "Well, I see you're a bright ray of sunshine this evening."

Snorting, Emma shook her head.

"Em, what's going on?" Abi asked, her voice serious.

Looking out her living room window, Emma just zoned out for a moment before answering, "I don't know."

Abi felt awful for her friend and said, "Tell me what's happened."

So, after a minute of huffing, Emma spilled it out. How they parted ways after the trip without a word, how he didn't call her, how he pretended to "save" her at the club, and how the misunderstanding with Dave happened.

After the whole mess was out, she sat down because she was physically exhausted.

Listening, Abi knew what she would've said to anyone else but Emma. She happened to be quite familiar with the experience since it just happened to her a few months ago.

Of course, explaining love to Emma would have no impact. Emma didn't budge unless she felt she was in charge. So Abi was just a quiet ear for her friend……for now.

"So what do I do?" Emma asked when Abi neglected to say anything after her story.

Abi cleared her throat and returned the question with one of her own, "What do you want to do?"

Frustrated, Emma snapped, "Don't try that psycho-babble bullshit on me, Abi!"

Understanding Emma's predicament, Abi knew she should tread slowly, and said, "Em, it's simple. If you want to spend time with him, do it."

Snorting again, Emma shook her head, "You wouldn't be saying that if you saw the look of disgust on his face when he saw Dave and me."

Not knowing what to say, Abi sighed. She wished she could just prescribe something but there was no cure for falling in love……thank goodness.

Braedon showed up for softball practice and was not looking forward to seeing Dave. The two men were friends but Braedon wanted to punch him in the face, repeatedly, for moving in on Emma.

He parked at the softball field and got out to get his bag.

The practice was already going when he got up to the fence that surrounded the field. He saw a few guys he worked with and said hello but changed his shoes and stretched out with his bat.

A few minutes later, the group on the field was coming in and Dave was with them. He spotted Braedon and wanted to apologize for the misunderstanding on Sunday.

"Richards," Dave called out as he neared the bench.

Braedon nodded in greeting but didn't say anything.

Not understanding that his friend was angry, Dave said, "Hey I wanted to say no hard feelings."

What the hell? Did this guy think he would just move in on Emma and it was okay? Not missing a beat, Braedon turned away so Dave wouldn't see the look of murder in his eyes.

Grabbing a bat, Dave didn't realize how much he pissed off Braedon, so he said, "Emma told me you misunderstood but I'm sure she explained. Had to get her a new coffeemaker after I broke the one at her place on Sunday."

The words Dave was saying were sinking in and Braedon turned to face him.

"Can't believe how clumsy I am for dropping it on the floor and spilling it all over my shirt," Dave said jokingly.

Dawning came slowly and, along with it, came a hefty pile of guilt. Before he could be sure, he needed to know some more.

Walking over to where Dave stood, Braedon asked, "So you didn't sleep over?"

Looking surprised, Dave answered, "Didn't Emma explain this? I went over to help her with some yard work and spilled coffee on my shirt so she told me to put it in the washer. She was upstairs getting dressed when you came to the door."

Damn! Damn! Damn! Braedon felt about two feet tall now. He had misunderstood and, on top of that, didn't give Emma the chance to explain.

Chapter 21

Tuesday was better for Emma, she felt a little relieved since talking to Abi. Just getting it out and sharing with her friend went a long way in helping her reconcile the situation.

It really came down to the fact that Braedon misunderstood a situation. He chose not to listen so it was his loss. She wouldn't contact him again. She was worth the time it took to listen and if any man thought differently, then he wasn't worth her time!

She went into work and was her usual efficient self.

After a morning spent in meetings, Emma was required to do a "Dog and Pony show." Really, it was a demonstration for some school kids and their teachers.

They got together some different exhibits and allowed the kids to climb into a Crash Crew truck and look at a helicopter. Pretty routine stuff and, usually, Emma didn't mind it.

Today, however, proved to be tough. Probably because, instead of one of the Staff Sgt.'s from Crash Crew, their spokesperson was none other than a Master Sgt. Richards.

Emma acknowledged him with a nod but that was it. She stood to the side mainly and just made sure no one wandered off and answered questions.

But, every few minutes, she found her eyes seeking him out.

He was very good too, dammit! He spoke loud enough to be heard but in simple terms so the kids could easily understand him.

His southern drawl came through and it made him endearing.

She noticed a few of the teachers whispering and smiling like women on the prowl. They didn't stand a chance with him!

Frustrated, because she was spending way too much time being preoccupied by a man that didn't want anything to do with her, Emma turned around and headed into the building.

Braedon saw her go into the Airfield Ops building and sighed on the inside. His nerves were on full alert since he came over for the demonstration. It wasn't his responsibility but he found himself asking the Staff Sgt. assigned if he minded being relieved for it. If it gave him time with Emma, then it was worth it.

But once he got set up and the kids started filing out, he felt his gut tighten and his nerves build. He had no idea what to say to her. 'I'm sorry,' wasn't going to enough in this situation.

He shook himself mentally and tried to concentrate on the questions the kids shot his way.

Emma got a drink of water and looked at her watch. They would wrap this up in a few minutes so she needed to get herself together.

She walked outside just in time to say good bye to the kids and accept the thanks from the teachers. After they were escorted back to their buses, she went back out to where the displays were.

Customarily, she went around and thanked all of the participants. Having a good rapport with the different squadrons and sections of Airfield Operations made for a much easier work environment.

She thanked everyone and finally came up to where Braedon was standing next to the Crash Crew P-19. He was talking to the crew so Emma held back until he shut the door and they were driving the vehicle back over in front of Crash Crew.

He turned around and Emma was prepared for the look of disgust she noticed the last couple of days. Instead, he greeted her with a smile and she was caught off balance. Damn!

"Thank you for including us, Master Gunnery Sgt. Cantrell," Braedon said to her.

He looked at the quick flash of surprise and felt even worse for being so hard on her.

Tilting her chin up in a sign of confidence, Emma nodded and replied, "Thank you, Master Sgt. Richards."

She turned and walked away, feeling his eyes on her back the whole way.

Thank goodness the afternoon was light. Emma was exhausted and only smiled when her boss let her go early.

She got out to her car in record time and threw her bag in haphazardly in an attempt to get the heck out of there.

The drive home was easy since school was still in session and the afternoon traffic hadn't started up yet. Her home welcomed her and she plopped down on the sofa without even changing out of her cammies and fell asleep almost immediately.

She dreamed......of Eryn and Kathrine and their babies, of Abi getting married, and of Braedon. He was trying to say something but she couldn't understand it. She was yelling at him to speak up when she startled awake.

Someone was at the door.

Groggily getting up, Emma wiped her eyes and walked to the front door. The afternoon sun was low in the sky and started to cast shadows in the room. She was thinking about turning on a light and peeked through the peephole. No one was there.

Frowning, Emma opened the door and was shocked by what she saw.

There, on her stoop, was a cellophane wrapped package. Emma looked up and down the street and didn't see anyone. She picked up the package and smiled.

Going back inside, Emma set down the package on the bar in the kitchen.

She greedily ripped off the colored cellophane and laughed at what she saw.

The "package" wasn't a package at all. It was a black cowboy hat that was tipped upside down to make it a basket of sorts. Inside it was boxes of her favorite candy and, in the middle, was a CD.

She picked up the case and read it.

Emma,

Please accept this lame attempt at impressing you as my apology for being a first rate jackass. My momma raised me better and the Marine Corps trained me better. I should have listened but I was so jealous, I probably looked like a leprechaun.

Emma laughed and read on.

Don't be mad, but I had to call Mitch, who put me in touch with Chase, who put me in touch with Eryn and she gave me a list of your favorite candy and your favorite music. Listen to it and think of me.

Sincerely Sorry,

Braedon

Tears were streaming down Emma's face. She was torn between being pissed that her friends gave out information that was tantamount to state secrets and wanting to kiss Braedon for being so thoughtful and inventive.

She walked over to her stereo and loaded the CD. The music started and she laughed.

The first song was a song that said, "I'm sorry." She sat down and listened to the entire CD. Each song was about making up or being sorry for not. The fact that he took the time to find the songs and put them on a CD, made Emma feel better than any flowers ever could.

Getting up, Emma walked over to the counter and picked up her phone. She sent a text to Braedon that simply said,

Apology Accepted.

Braedon's phone went off and he quickly picked it up. He saw the text from Emma and sighed in relief. It was a gamble but he figured Emma wasn't the average flower and candy kind of girl. She would need a bigger statement, especially when groveling was involved.

Smiling, he sent one back.

Since you're feeling so gracious, would dinner be out of the question?

Emma got the text and was going to reply when she had a thought. Grabbing the hat, she started toward her room and typed a quick reply.

Here at 7.

Looking at his watch and seeing he only had about 45 minutes, he went in to shower. He didn't bother to answer her text.

At 6:45 Emma was pretty sure she had everything set. The sun was dipping low in the sky, about to say goodnight.

More's the better as far as she was concerned. She was out on the back patio lighting candles. The effect was like a glowing wonderland. Taking off her cover up, she stepped into the pool and waited.

Braedon pulled up in front of Emma's place at 6:55pm. He'd showered and changed into a nice shirt and jeans. She didn't say where they were going so he hoped his choice was acceptable.

He got out of the car and was going to knock when he saw the note taped to the front door.

Braedon,

We're having dinner on the back patio, please come in and make yourself at home. I'll be down in a minute.

Emma

Smiling, Braedon opened the door and went inside.

There was a corner lamp on in the living room but that was it. The house seemed to be settled in for the night and was really quiet. He listened and could hear music in the distance.

Going through the kitchen, Braedon smiled when he saw the cartons of Chinese food on the counter. Dinner, he supposed. He stepped out onto the back patio and almost fell over with what he saw.

There were candles all around the pool area and made it look magical.

Emma was in the pool, on a round blow up ring. She was wearing the cowboy hat he got her and absolutely nothing else.

"Hello, Braedon," Emma said slowly.

Braedon was trying to process the situation. She was there, in the pool, naked, and looked like some sort of dream. He had to mentally kick himself to get words to come out of his mouth.

He managed a weak, "Hi," and cringed at how odd it sounded.

Emma knew she was taking a calculated risk but, judging by Braedon's expression, she'd done it right. Luckily, one of her neighbors was out of town and the other was older and had awful eyesight so she figured this was a fairly safe plan.

Noticing that he still wasn't saying anything or moving, she started to wonder so she asked, "Are you okay?"

Nodding, Braedon took a couple of steps closer to the pool, "I'm just blown away by this gorgeous water nymph in the pool who, if I'm not mistaken, is ready to be rescued."

Liking the game, she answered, "Well, you are a fireman so I'm sure you're in the habit of rescuing naked women all the time."

Braedon shook his head no, "Not women who are as beautiful and sexy as you are." His voice carried the edge of desire pulsing through his veins.

He stopped at the edge of the pool as she made her way toward him.

Emma had heard those words before from guys who were just being flirty and from men she was involved with, but she never heard them quite the way Braedon said them. It caused her belly to flip inside.

Once she reached the edge of the pool where the stairs were, she gracefully hopped out of inflatable ring. The water cooled her heated skin. It felt erotic for her to walk out of the pool to meet him.

Chapter 22

His eyes never left hers as she walked over to him. He would've rather taken her out of the pool but his limbs were weighed down in place.

Standing in front of him, exposed in every way, Emma looked up into his eyes. She saw the desire, and knew she would since she felt it too. There was something else there that puzzled her but now wasn't the time to figure it all out. He was here and that was enough.

Reaching over, Emma took his hand into hers and lifted it to her lips.

When she touched him, he was lost. There were no more coherent thoughts, it was all about feeling her skin against his. He stepped closer and leaned down to kiss her.

Emma welcomed his lips. They were light on hers as if Braedon was letting her set the tone.

The kiss was deep, Emma's tongue delving into his mouth for more. She groaned when he pulled her against him.

"I'm getting your clothes wet," she mumbled with a smile.

Braedon growled, "Woman, I don't care what you do to them. I need you."

His words almost made her buckle over with physical pain in her chest. She didn't know what it was about him that made her swim in chaos internally but it was a confusingly pleasurable pain.

Kissing again, Braedon reached down and lifted her up by her bottom, her legs swung around him and clamped together, which brought them together more intimately.

If he didn't get her upstairs, he was going to be really embarrassed. Turning around, his eyes open so he could see, Braedon walked them inside the house.

Emma just kept kissing him. When she needed to breathe, she moved her lips down over his chin and to his neck. His cologne smelled very much like him, male and tender.

After a slow start, Braedon was able to make it up the stairs.

He asked her, "Where's your bedroom?" in between kisses.

Emma nodded to the end of the hallway and smiled. She'd stopped kissing him and watched his face as he walked, with her wrapped around him, to the bedroom. His face looked set as if he were on an important mission. His eyes were dark and looked almost wild. Emma was glad he was reacting like she was; it put them on equal ground.

Braedon reached the bed and gently put Emma down on it. He backed up only far enough to start taking off his clothes. Frustration peaked when he started fumbling with the buttons on his shirt.

Smiling, Emma got up on her knees and helped him unbutton his shirt. She didn't say anything, just immersed herself in the way he felt under her fingers.

When the buttons of his shirt were undone, she yanked the fabric up and out of his jeans. Now she had unfettered access to his chest and ran her fingers up and down it.

"If you don't stop that, this is going to end pretty much here and now," Braedon said tightly.

Emma smiled and responded, "Oh, I think you've got it all under control, Master Sgt."

Watching Emma, kneeling on the bed and touching him, Braedon wondered how she could say his rank and make it sound so damn sexy.

Leaning down again, Braedon captured her lips with his, nipping at the swollen flesh as he began making love to her with his mouth.

His kisses were like a drug to Emma's system, they made her heart race and her brain fog until she wasn't sure she was actually conscious anymore. Sensations layered up so quickly, her mind couldn't process it. In defeat, she let her head fall back and gave Braedon access to all of her.

Braedon kissed her while undoing his pants. He slid them down and managed to kick off his shoes in record time.

Guiding Emma down so she was laying on the bed, Braedon slid onto the bed and lay beside her.

He ran his fingers over her thigh and cupped her intimately.

Groaning, Emma tried to keep her orgasm from coming over her. How the hell could she be so ready when all he'd done was kiss her and barely touch her?

Smiling, Braedon could see she was almost there and wanted to give her pleasure before he satisfied his own needs.

Using his fingers, he slid two inside of her, moaning when his finger felt how hot and wet she was. He leaned down and captured her nipple in his mouth as he slowly rubbed her already hardened nub.

'NO!' Emma was saying on the inside. She felt the wave starting and was helpless to stop it from washing over her with a force that took the breath out of her lungs.

"Yes, baby," Braedon whispered against her skin as she went over the edge.

Emma arched up and accepted the pulsating heat sweep across her skin and melt her insides until she was a puddle of sensations.

She managed to open her eyes and look up to see Braedon half leaning over her, a wicked smile on his face.

"You look awfully smug," she said.

Braedon nodded, "I suppose I do but you sure do look like the sexiest thing I've ever seen when you are in the middle of an orgasm."

She reached up and cupped his cheek with her palm. She wasn't embarrassed by his words; why should she be? They made the decision to have sex and she wasn't one of those women who acted shy. She liked how he made her feel and wasn't ashamed to say it.

Raising her head, Emma kissed him slowly. Her senses were returning so she wanted to return the favor. Before he knew what she was doing, Emma moved and flipped him over. She was straddling his thighs, her hands splayed over his chest.

'She's quick,' Braedon thought as she reversed their positions. He certainly didn't mind, looking up at her as she moved against him. He thought she was what the great writers wrote about and the great artists painted. Her skin almost glowed in the moonlight that snuck into the room.

Her hair was loose since she lost the cowboy hat when he laid her on the bed. It was long and thick and moved over her shoulders as she moved over him.

"I want to return the favor," Emma whispered to him as she moved over his hard shaft.

Her own body was responding much quicker than she anticipated so it was difficult to keep her mind in gear.

Braedon didn't answer, only clasped his hands behind his head. He wouldn't fight the pleasure.

Seeing him look so cocky made Emma determined. She slid off of him and moved so she was kneeling between his legs.

Braedon started to sit up and she pushed him back down.

She liked him being surprised, it made her want him even more.

Leaning down, Emma wrapped her hands around his erection and playfully flicked her tongue across the tip of it.

Braedon sucked in a sharp breath, trying to think of anything that would help make it so he didn't embarrass himself in front of Emma.

Taking him into her mouth fully, Emma watched him. He was fighting it, she could see it, but she wasn't one to be outdone; in the bedroom, or anywhere else for that matter.

She loved the feeling of his hardness in her mouth. She reveled in the responses he gave. His back arching, his muscles tensing, it all made her body tingle in delight.

Knowing he wouldn't last much longer at this rate, Braedon grabbed her arms and pulled her up and over so she was pinned halfway beneath him on the bed.

"Why did you stop me?" Emma asked him.

Braedon smiled and said, "Because I want you to be with me when I explode."

The words sent shivers through her body.

She nodded and whispered, "I thought maybe I wasn't doing it right."

Tilting his head, Braedon glared at her.

"I think you know exactly what you're doing every minute of every day, Emma," he said and then kissed her deeply.

She sunk into the kiss, allowing him to take over her body with his loving manipulations and wondered how he had her pegged so well.

Danette Fogarty

They kissed and explored one another with hands, as new lovers do, and finally, Braedon positioned himself above her. She was arching up trying to pull him down so they would be joined intimately.

Braedon looked down at Emma and smiled softly as he said, "Just wait."

Asking Emma to be patient was like asking Mother Nature to stop making rain; it wasn't going to happen.

She watched Braedon and sighed deeply when he slid inside of her. She wrapped her legs around his waist and wondered why they fit together so perfectly.

Starting slowly, Braedon concentrated on her. If he even gave a thought to how incredible she felt, surrounding him with her heat, he would explode. He wanted them to climax together.

The pressure inside Emma was so exquisite. She knew Braedon was waiting for her and she so wanted to please him. Wanting his pleasure before hers was actually erotic in and of itself, she found the clawing ache take root low in her belly and start to spread.

"Braedon, come with me," she hissed as she started the crescendo of sensations.

His face frozen in sexual concentration, Braedon sped up his pace and within seconds, met her on the crest of desire.

He yelled out, "Emma!" and felt his body crash into a tailspin of crazy feelings.

Emma embraced the orgasm and smiled because she knew he met it with her.

Braedon was careful to lay down beside her as exhaustion took over his body. He pulled her into his arms and held her against him as the last remnants of light went out of the candle that was burning beside the bed.

Emma woke up slowly. She smelled something so good and her stomach was growling with hunger but her mind was content with the sleep she found.

She felt the bed move and opened her eyes. Squinting in the light given off by the bedside lamp, she made out Braedon sitting on the side of the bed, shirtless, and holding Chinese food containers.

"What time is it?" she asked as she sat up.

Braedon smiled, she looked gorgeous even when she was just waking up.

He glanced at the bedside clock and answered, "About 10:30."

Emma nodded and took the carton from him. He had heated up the food and it tasted wonderful. She peeked over the container to see him eating greedily.

"Worked up an appetite, huh?" Emma asked slyly.

Nodding, Braedon smiled and asked, "Didn't you?"

Huffing, Emma answered, "Uh, yeah!" and laughed.

They ate their food, sharing a bite here and there, until they were full. Braedon took the containers downstairs and told her to stay put.

Sitting in her bed, she dutifully followed his direction. She was leaning up against the headboard, her sheet pulled up around her breasts. Not that she was all about propriety but it seemed like the right thing to do.

Thinking about their lovemaking, Emma closed her eyes and was going over the way he made her feel when he came back into the room.

Braedon found her sitting on the bed, daydreaming.

"You look deep in thought," he said.

Emma opened her eyes and smiled sweetly, and answered, "Just thinking about what you do to me."

"And what is that?" Braedon asked.

He started unbuttoning his jeans. He'd thrown them on when he went downstairs to heat up the food.

Watching him, Emma said, "You make me want you."

The directness of her words hit his gut like a sledgehammer and drove his body into overdrive. He couldn't resist her and he sure didn't want to.

Kicking off his jeans, Braedon said, "Well, ma'am, I aim to do that," in an overly exaggerated southern drawl.

Laughing, Emma pushed at him as he laid down beside her and said, "But not when you do that."

"Understood," Braedon answered her.

He pulled her to him and began kissing her once again. He was pretty sure that he would never tire of kissing her. He was pretty sure he would never tire of her......ever.

Chapter 23

The rest of the week was spent much like that night. Emma would invite him over and they would have dinner and then make love until both of them were exhausted.

On Friday night, Braedon had a softball game and asked Emma to come.

She said yes immediately but, now that she was at the ball park, she was reluctant to walk over to the stands.

This was the first time they would be out in public as a couple. The wedding weekend didn't count because it was across the country. Emma was always so careful about publicly dating someone and always planned it out so carefully. With Braedon she said something without thinking about the consequences.

She sat in her car and stared at the ball diamond. People were laughing and walking over and she stayed in her car, frozen in place.

A tap on her window had her jumping. She saw it was Dave so she put the window down.

"Hey," Dave said and pointed to the ball field before asking her, "you coming to the game?"

Thinking that she was no baby, Emma smiled and nodded.

Dave invited her to his games all the time. She forgot that little detail too when she said yes to Braedon about coming. Would Dave be pissed that she was coming to see Braedon and not him?

Standing aside, Dave waited for Emma to get out of the car, then walked with her toward the ball field.

"About time you came," he said as they walked up beside the stands, "even if it wasn't to see me," he added and smiled at the shocked look on Emma's face.

Watching Dave walk off, Emma couldn't help but laugh. Friends can always make life bearable.

Emma snapped out of her thoughts and started up the bleachers to find a place to sit.

Braedon was warming up for the game but kept looking toward the bleachers to see if Emma showed up. He wondered if she would. Truth be told, he was surprised when she agreed to come. With Emma he figured that she was the one used to calling the shots so she wouldn't want to break that particular habit.

This week was one of the best ones he could remember. After Tuesday night, he was shaken to the core with his feelings for her. So, when she texted him

Wednesday and asked if he wanted to come over for a "sleepover" he was shocked but said yes immediately.

She grilled some fish and they had a great dinner. He wasn't sure he was actually staying until she made the comment while they were cleaning up the dinner dishes.

Then last night he offered to bring over a pizza and asked her to come to watch his game. She agreed to both without hesitation.

But when he arrived here tonight, he knew nothing was concrete. Spending time in bed was one thing but spending time in public was something else altogether. He learned that Emma cherished her privacy and wasn't in the mind to give it up easily.

He noticed Dave coming out onto the field and raised a hand in greeting. Once he returned his gaze back to the bleachers, he saw her sitting down.

'She showed!' he thought to himself.

The game was good and, in no time, Emma found herself being caught up in the crowd. She joined in the yelling when the umpire called a strike for their team and booed with the others during another close call.

Baseball was fun and she liked to play as a kid. That was, until her mother decided she was to act like a lady and entered her into the most atrocious beauty pageants.

Not wanting to think about her past, Emma re-focused on the game going on before her.

Braedon was up to bat. Two outs and it was the last at bat for their team. The score was tied but there was a runner on first and second base.

She cheered with the others for Braedon and was so excited that her fists were clenched on her lap.

The first pitch and it was….a strike. Emma stood and yelled, "Booooo!"

The second pitch came and it was….a ball.

"Come on, Richards!" she yelled loudly.

Braedon could hear her because he turned to face her and shot her a wink.

Emma held her breath as the third pitch was thrown. She squeezed her eyes shut until she heard the unmistakable sound of the ball and bat colliding…..thwack!

Jumping up, Emma screamed as Braedon took off running. The runner on second rounded third base and easily touched home plate. The runner on first was rounding third base when the ball was thrown from far left field up to the pitcher.

The runner was coming and the pitcher threw the ball to the catcher.

Everyone held their breath as the runner slid and the catcher tagged him and it felt like forever for the umpire to say………. "Safe!"

The crowd erupted and the game was over.

Emma waited where she was as people made their way down the bleachers and towards the parking lot. She watched the teams as they shook hands on the field before retreating to their respective benches.

She could see how happy Braedon was as his teammates congratulated him with pats on the back. She was happy for him too but had other congratulatory activities in mind.

Braedon glanced up into the bleachers and saw people filing down. He assumed that Emma would come down and meet him near the bench his team was assigned to. He accepted the "good job" comments from his team and was glad they won. The other team was one of the best in the league.

After getting his bag together, he walked around the fence and saw Emma, still sitting where she was during the game. She was wearing a smile but there was something in her eyes that looked almost devious.

He stood at the bottom of the bleachers and called up to her, "Are you ready to go home?"

Staying where she was, Emma replied, "I was waiting to see what kind of offer I got."

Lord, she was a handful! He smiled, and said, "This is the only offer you're going to get tonight, I'm afraid."

Tilting her head, Emma studied him. The comment was almost self-deprecating. It caused Emma's temper to flare and she fought to tamp down on it.

She stood up and slowly made her way down the bleachers until she hopped down and was facing him.

"Why, are you afraid?" she asked him seriously, "I'm not afraid."

Emma's knack for turning comments over and every which way made him want to kiss the look of smugness off of her face. Maybe one of these days he would do just that.

Taking her hand in his, Braedon said, "Well then, let's go."

Hand in hand, they walked toward the parking lot.

Saturday morning was usually reserved for errands Emma didn't do during the week. She kept a list on a pad of paper in the kitchen and grimaced when she saw it. The paper was half full and would take her most of the afternoon to complete.

Out of habit, she woke up early and came downstairs to turn the coffee maker on. Braedon was still sleeping and she left him to it. After all, she had worn him out so he needed his rest.

Still smiling a few minutes later, Emma was leaning against the kitchen counter and lost in her thoughts when Braedon came into the room.

"That's a smile a man could come to appreciate," he said in his now-familiar southern drawl.

Emma noticed that it was more pronounced when he first woke up or when he was mad.

Another tidbit she needed to put in her mental "Braedon file."

Walking over to Emma, Braedon leaned over and kissed her on the lips before grabbing a mug for himself.

She handed him the coffee pot and went to rinse out her mug in the sink before saying, "Hurry up and drink up so you can go home. I've got a ton of errands today."

Even though she leaned over and kissed him before heading upstairs to get ready, Braedon couldn't shake the feeling that he'd been systematically dismissed.

Not that he didn't have his own obligations that he needed to keep, it was just the way she said some things.

Brushing it off, Braedon finished his coffee then headed upstairs to get the rest of his clothes.

The afternoon passed in a flurry and Emma finally rolled into the house after 5pm. She was tired and hungry and loaded down with dry cleaning and groceries.

After she put the food away and went upstairs to hang up her clothes, she checked her phone for the hundredth time. She fully expected a call, or at least a text from Braedon. She assumed they would spend the evening together and possibly tomorrow too. But she hadn't heard a word from him since they parted ways earlier.

Remembering that communication went both ways, she called him and left a message asking him to call her.

Two hours later, when she hadn't heard from him, she was mad. In an effort to take her mind off of him, she called Eryn.

The phone rang twice before Eryn picked up with a, "Hello, now I'm good enough to talk to."

Emma laughed and answered, "Yes."

"Fine," Eryn said and started with, "I'm as big as a house and you are skinny and gorgeous, I'm sure."

Feeling bad for Eryn, Emma responded, "Actually, I've got some thyroid thing that caused me to gain fifty pounds."

Rolling her eyes, Eryn sat down on the patio and propped her now swelling feet up on a nearby chair.

"I doubt it," Eryn pouted.

Shaking her head, Emma asked, "What does Chase say about your blossoming figure?"

Eryn snorted, "Oh he says, 'You're beautiful,' and all that other crap but I feel like a blimp that's being inflated."

Emma laughed, she always liked Eryn's sense of humor.

They talked for almost an hour and Emma filled in details Eryn hadn't gotten from Abi. They laughed and talked about Katherine's same complaints. Emma doubted that either of them were as large as the Empire State Building but she did her due diligence and fussed. They were all supposed to meet up in two weeks for the baby shower in Virginia and she would see for herself how "big" they were.

After she hung up with Eryn, Emma smiled as she collected laundry to throw in the washer. She threw it in a basket and went downstairs to the laundry room.

She started sorting the load and came across one of Braedon's t-shirts. He must've left it by accident. Lifting up the shirt and holding it to her face, she could smell him. She stood there, next to the washer until she mentally shook herself.

What the hell! She didn't smell shirts! She didn't sit around waiting for a guy that obviously had better things to do than call her!

Shoving the shirt inside the washer, Emma went into the kitchen and picked up her phone.

Within an hour she was ready to meet up with some of her friends downtown. Out of habit, she glanced at her phone and saw a missed call from Braedon. 'Well, too bad,' she thought to herself and walked out of the house.

Braedon spent the weekend doing some volunteer work Jason roped him into for a kids' charity in Temecula, California. He was glad to help but missed Emma while he was doing it.

Jason even commented on more than one occasion that he would, "Drop the damn phone if he kept checking it while he was working."

Glaring at Jason was quickly becoming one of his habits. They were building a pretty large playground set that was designed for the organization personally and took about ten people two days to get it assembled.

He would probably be in a better mood if Emma called him back. He called her yesterday to ask her if she wanted to help out today. Maybe they could grab some dinner afterward with Jason and Kathy or something. But, Emma never called.

There were things he understood about her but he didn't have to like them.

Like her insistence that she be the one to call the shots. Or like the fact that she could sleep with him then dismiss him like he didn't mean a cotton-pickin thing to her.

Two hours later, the playground was done and Braedon was on his way home, alone.

Sunday evening Emma was watching a movie when her phone rang. She paused the movie and looked at the caller ID to see that it was Braedon.

"Hey there," she answered with a smile.

"Where were you?" Braedon asked with a sharp tone.

Emma immediately knew he was looking for a fight. His tone was almost accusatory. She refused to take the bait.

Sighing, Emma answered, "I'm fine, how are you doing this weekend?"

His frustration getting the better of him, Braedon snapped, "I'm pissed, Emma!"

"Obviously," Emma responded dryly.

Her tone only added to his already inflated anger.

Trying to calm down, Braedon waited before answering, "I thought since we spent the week together, that this weekend we'd do the same."

'And there it is,' Emma thought to herself. Why is it that people automatically thought that sleeping together meant commitment? Not that she took it lightly but neither of them professed any kind of love.

Very calmly, Emma said, "Braedon, you thought wrong."

Braedon couldn't decide if he was more upset by the fact that Emma didn't call him back or by the fact that she was so nonchalant about them. Deciding that he needed time to think about this, Braedon calmed down enough to be polite.

He cleared his throat and said, "You're right. I apologize. I looked at us making love for four nights straight and, I guess mistakenly, thought that meant something to both of us. I guess it only meant something to me, Emma. Goodnight."

Emma didn't even have a chance to respond before she heard the phone click and the dial tone buzzed in her ear.

Setting the phone back down, she turned the movie on and stared at the screen. For some reason, when the movie ended, she didn't remember a thing about it.

Chapter 24

Emma spent the next week trying to figure out what to do about Braedon. He hadn't called her since Sunday and that surprised her. She assumed that, once he calmed down, he'd see she had a point.

By the following Saturday, she was going stir crazy at the house. Nothing held any appeal. She had a list of errands and didn't have any inclination to do them. Food wasn't interesting and nothing held her attention for very long.

The following weekend she would fly to Virginia to see the girls and Emma was relieved to get away. Had it only been a month since she and Braedon went to Katherine and Mitch's wedding? How did the time fly so fast?

She was about to go out to the garage and do some work out with the Heavy Bag when her phone rang.

"Aha," she said with a smile, sure it was Braedon.

Tapping the accept button, Emma hurriedly said, "Hello."

A delicate voice answered, "Hello, Emma."

Emma sat down at the bar in her kitchen. Hearing from her mother threw her. She didn't know what to say.

"I got your cell number from Christina," Cynthia Cantrell said.

Still not speaking, Emma silently cursed her youngest sister for her blabbing.

Taking a breath, Cynthia spoke up, "I'm sure you're surprised to hear from me."

That was the understatement of the century in Emma's mind. Her mother spent most of Emma's youth parading her in and out of every beauty pageant within a thousand miles of their home in Indiana. Her father worked two to three jobs to support Cynthia's dream of making their daughter "somebody."

If Cynthia would have had her own way, Emma would have competed at the State level and, hopefully, gone on to compete for Miss America.

Emma always indulged her mother's dreams. For a while, she even thought they might be her own dreams. That was, until she turned sixteen.

Suddenly, high school and boys were more important than the beauty pageants. Emma just wanted to do the normal things that teenagers did but Cynthia wouldn't stand for it. Mother and daughter were suddenly on opposing sides.

Emma started refusing to go to beauty pageants and Cynthia tried to take away anything away from Emma she thought would change her daughter's mind.

Out of desperation, Emma went to her father and asked him about his time in the Marine Corps. He had served four years before marrying her mother and spoke highly of the people he met. He talked of how everyone, men and women, were treated the same. In a uniform, you held a special kind of pride.

Emma made the decision to join and waited until her seventeenth birthday before going to her father and begging him to sign for her to enlist.

Tim Cantrell went down to the recruiter's office and signed for his daughter to join up. Neither of them realized what that decision would do to their family.

The next fight Emma had with her mother, she tossed the enlistment papers at her and waited for Cynthia to read them. Emma couldn't have predicted the pain her actions caused her mother.

Cynthia looked at her daughter and husband and told them both that she wouldn't speak to them again.

The next day, Cynthia was gone. She packed up and left her family to go back to her hometown several hundred miles away, leaving her father to deal with four daughters on his own.

The pain of that rejection still hit Emma at the oddest moments. Now she could see how wrong they all were, but at the time, she was just a kid who needed her mom to see that she had her own dreams.

Cynthia's voice permeated through Emma's memories and brought her back to the present.

"I know I said I wouldn't speak to you again but I think eighteen years is long enough," Cynthia said quietly.

A tear ran down Emma's cheek, "Maybe," she answered because that's all she could muster.

Cynthia smiled. Her daughter, like her husband, was slow to forgive. Probably because she'd hurt them deeply. Guilt filled up her chest once again.

Emma asked, "Have you talked to Dad?"

Smiling, Cynthia answered, "Yes, we've been talking for about six months now."

The news surprised Emma. Neither her sisters nor her dad said anything to her and she spoke to all of them before leaving for Katherine and Mitch's wedding.

Her parents never divorced. Emma always wondered why they stayed married even though they didn't speak. She asked her dad that question ten years earlier and he said, "Because I love her."

Emma thought they were both a little nuts but it was their life.

"What do you want, Mom?" Emma asked coolly.

Hearing her daughter say, "Mom," brought tears to Cynthia's eyes.

She answered, "I'm calling to make amends, Emma."

Tears sliding freely down her cheeks now, Emma responded with, "That's a good thing."

Emma walked over to the sofa in her living room, grabbed a box of tissues from the end table, and started listening to her mom.

Braedon was helping Jason with inventory at Bullz on Saturday morning, a frown creasing his brow.

Emma didn't call him all week and she dismissed him.....again. Dammit!!!!!!

Jason watched his brother and wondered how he could be such an idiot. Anybody could see he was at least half in love with Emma. In all the years he'd known his brother, he'd never seen him act like this. Braedon would look better if someone kicked the crap out of him. 'If this is what love did,' Jason thought to himself, 'count me out!'

Calling over to Braedon, Jason asked, "What's the count on that cabinet, bro?"

Braedon looked down at the tally sheet he had in front of him and realized he didn't enter any numbers on it.

He tried to cover up by saying, "I put the numbers in the wrong places, I have to recount."

"If you're not going to help, then just go home," Jason snapped.

Slamming the clipboard down on the counter, Braedon shouted back, "I'm here!"

Shaking his head, Jason went into the other room and mumbled, "Maybe you're here physically, but not mentally."

Emma hung up with her mom after talking for almost three hours. She was emotionally exhausted but that conversation was long past due. Feeling a little excited, Emma started to call Braedon. When she realized what she was doing, she stopped. He didn't know about her parents and the situation.

'And whose fault is that?' she asked herself, mentally.

Putting down her phone, Emma picked up her keys and purse and left the house.

Braedon finished the inventory with Jason just in time for the bar to open. He felt a little guilty that it took them so long. It was clearly because Braedon was distracted and thinking about Emma.

At least his brother didn't judge him too harshly. Braedon was thankful for his family and their support. His mom had been asking about coming out for a visit and he should really have her come out soon. Maybe she could meet Emma?

Kathy came into the bar and interrupted his thoughts.

"Hey there," she said brightly to Braedon.

Smiling, Braedon returned with, "Hey there, yourself. You look nice."

Blushing, Kathy smiled shyly and answered, "Thank you."

Braedon was about to say something when Jason came out from the back room. He stopped and stared at Kathy.

"Jason," Kathy said coolly and went to put her purse in the back room.

Watching Jason as he watched Kathy, Braedon wondered if his brother knew he was in love with Kathy. A shame if he didn't since she'd been in love with him forever. 'Poor guy,' Braedon thought.

Emma walked in the door and took her bags over to the counter. After dutifully putting away the groceries, she went upstairs and changed into her swimsuit. She walked out onto the patio and dialed Eryn's number before sitting down on a chaise.

"Hello there," Eryn answered.

Emma smiled and asked, "Are you busy?"

Chuckling, Eryn said, "Only growing a human being inside of me, what's up?"

"Nice," Emma commented.

Eryn noticed something in Emma's voice and asked, "What happened?"

It was uncanny and a little scary that Eryn knew when something was up. It was one of the things that made her Emma's go-to friend.

Sighing, Emma said, "My mother called me."

Eryn stopped mid-step. This was a big deal! Sticking her head into the living room to get Chase's attention, she mouthed "Emma," and went into the study.

"I'm all ears," Eryn said once she settled down in the chair.

Taking a deep breath, Emma began, "She called to say she wanted to make amends."

Knowing that this was just the tip of a very large emotional iceberg, Eryn nodded and said, "Okay, and?"

"I was shocked," Emma said, then added, "And she and Dad have been talking for about six months."

Eryn's eyebrows shot up, "And you didn't know about that?"

Emma sighed, "No." She put her feet up underneath her on the sofa, "Neither Dad or Chris said anything."

Years earlier, Emma told Eryn about her parents and how her decision basically split them up. Eryn tried to assure her at the time that her parents made their own decisions and it wasn't Emma's fault.

Emma thought that she shouldn't be dependent on her looks and she wanted some semblance of normalcy. Her mother just wanted her to rely on her looks to be famous or some such thing.

Eryn knew that she and Abi and Katherine were pretty women but none of them had the striking looks that Emma was born with. Emma could easily be a model or actress, even now that she was in her late thirties. But it was the fact that Emma wasn't able to make the decision that was the crux of their family rift.

"Now what?" Eryn asked her friend.

Emma absently looked outside when she answered, "She wants to see me. She and Dad are getting together tomorrow and they are considering a trip out here next month."

'Whoa,' Eryn thought. This was big news.

Before Emma could say anything else, Eryn asked, "What does Braedon have to say about all this?"

The question threw Emma for a bit of a loop.

"Uh, he doesn't know about it," Emma answered.

Rolling her eyes, Eryn knew this was a problem. Emma didn't share. She was immensely private and, Eryn suspected, hadn't told Braedon much of anything about herself or her past.

Frowning, Emma said, "I know what you're going to say, but it never came up."

"Em, did it never come up or did you just not say anything?" Eryn asked, knowing the question would piss off Emma.

Shaking her head, Emma snapped, "It has nothing to do with him."

Defensive…..Eryn smiled and asked, "Are you still seeing him?"

Emma jumped up off the couch and started pacing, "I don't think so," she answered.

Confused.....Eryn thought that was interesting as well.

"Did you have a fight?" Eryn asked.

Plopping back down on the sofa, Emma mumbled, "Sort of."

'Oh, she's a goner,' Eryn thought.

Leaning back, as much as she could comfortably, Eryn said, "Tell Auntie Eryn all about it."

Emma smiled reluctantly and did just that.

Chapter 25

Emma sat in the airport on Thursday afternoon and frowned.

She'd received calls from Katherine's mother, Eryn, Abi, and even Mitch asking if Braedon was coming this weekend.

Originally, that was the plan. But now things were different. He didn't call her and she didn't call him. At least for her, it was a pride thing. If she called him first, he'd see that he had some influence on her. Emma swore that no one would ever have that kind of power over her.

That was why she never dated anyone longer than four months. After that, there was an expectation of a relationship. Emma needed the freedom to walk away.

Of course, now that she was talking to her mother again, she could see how much that whole situation played a part in her attitude toward relationships.

But, knowing it and doing something about it were two entirely different things.

Her phone rang and it was Abi. Hitting the accept button, she smiled and said, "What now!"

Smiling, Abi answered, "I'm here."

"In Virginia?" Emma asked.

"No," Abi said, "right behind you."

Turning around, Emma saw that Abi was standing a few feet away.

Jumping up, Emma yelled, "Ayyyyy!" and hugged her friend tightly.

Abi was up to date on what was going on, thanks to Eryn's loose lips. She knew she had a layover in California but changed flights so it was in San Diego and she could fly with Emma.

Standing back, Abi looked her friend over. Emma's makeup was expertly done, her hair lay soft around her shoulders, her clothes were beautiful, but there was a sadness in her eyes that Abi had never seen before now. Maybe Eryn's fears were right on?

"We'll be travel buddies," Abi said and walked with Emma back to her seat in the gate waiting area.

Emma laughed, "I'd like that."

Abi asked, "So how are things here?"

'Loaded question,' Emma thought to herself, but said, "Good."

Frowning, Abi said, "Bullshit, Em."

That was Abi, never one to pull too many punches.

"He doesn't call, I don't call, we're just being stubborn," Emma finally said.

Abi nodded and answered, "Not surprising."

Another good thing about Abi was her "less is more" use of words.

Their flight was announced and they each got their bags and put their conversations on hold for the time being.

The flight to Virginia was great as far as Emma was concerned. She and Abi talked about Eryn and Katherine, the babies, and a lot about Abi and Gav's wedding.

When Abi tried to ask about Braedon, Emma shut her down quickly. She didn't want him to interfere with her time with friends.

They landed and grabbed a rental car in short order. The baby shower was being held at a hotel banquet room with all the fixings. Emma and Abi were staying at a hotel near to where Katherine and Mitch lived so they went there first.

After checking in, they called Katherine and told her they were coming over.

Eryn and Chase arrived a couple of days earlier, using the time to visit with Eryn's parents before the festivities started.

As Abi drove to Mitch and Katherine's she said, "You know they're all going to ask."

Nodding, Emma answered, "I know."

"He wasn't good enough for you, Em, it's that simple," Abi said flippantly.

Emma turned to face her friend, her face set in stone, "That was uncalled for, Abigale," she ground out through clenched teeth.

Unaffected by her friend's increasing anger, Abi said, "No, Emma, it wasn't. He's not in your league."

Seething, Emma yelled, "He's better than any man you or I know!"

"I guess I'll have to take your word on that." Abi got out and turned away so Emma didn't see her smiling.

Emma systematically turned away from Abi and stared out the window of the car.

'What the hell does she know?' Emma thought to herself.

They pulled up in front of the house and Mitch came out to greet them.

He hugged Abi first and then turned to hug Emma. She looked mad but he didn't care and gathered her up into his arms.

Emma hugged Mitch hard. She was still mad about what Abi was saying and his hug did a good bit in helping her calm down. He was like a brother to her.

"Ladies," Mitch said, "the two queens are waiting inside for you to join them."

Laughing, Emma grabbed her purse and followed Abi inside.

Eryn and Katherine were standing inside, huge smiles on their faces.

Even though Eryn and Abi worked together, they hugged tightly and chatted about the baby.

"We're getting bigger," Eryn whined, "and, compared to Katherine, I look like a house."

Emma shook her head, "You do not; you just carry differently."

Eryn, Katherine, and Abi all stared at her.

Rolling her eyes, Emma said, "What!" and added, "It's not like I don't know what's going on."

All four of them broke out into giggles.

Katherine took them upstairs to see the nursery. Abi was gushing over the little clothes and diapers already arranged in the closet. Emma made, what she felt like, were appropriate noises. The truth was, Emma liked kids just fine; she just never considered having one of her own.

After the tour, the women went back downstairs and into the living room.

They talked about the babies, about husbands, about the upcoming wedding, and all sorts of things. The only thing they didn't talk about was Braedon.

Emma brought him up by saying, "Nobody's being nosy."

Abi chimed in, "You know how I feel."

Glaring at her friend, Emma didn't say anything.

Katherine asked, "How do you feel, Abi?"

"I told her he wasn't good enough for her," Abi said.

Emma responded with a slow, "Drop dead."

Eryn's eyebrows went up. She looked at Emma disapprovingly.

"Emma," she said tightly, "that was just Abi's opinion and I happen to share it."

Emma couldn't believe her ears. Her friends were actually saying that Braedon wasn't good enough? What the hell did they know about him? They'd met him for what? Two days?

Katherine nodded, "I'm afraid, Em, I may have to go with the other two on this one."

Standing up, Emma looked from Eryn to Abi and then from Abi to Katherine.

"Since when," she started, "did any of you have a say in who's good enough for me?"

The three of them stared at her and didn't answer.

Emma threw her hands up in frustration and walked out of the room.

Eryn turned to Abi and Katherine and said, "I hope he thanks us after this is all done with?"

Nodding, Katherine said, "I think he will."

Abi wanted to be as confident at Eryn and Katherine but she was afraid that this little plan of theirs would backfire and Emma would end up more hurt than she already was.

Emma walked into the kitchen to find Mitch preparing some lemonade.

"You look domestic," she said to him as she walked toward him.

Nodding, Mitch smiled, "Yep."

Sitting at the breakfast bar across from him, Emma asked, "Can I ask you a question?"

"Shoot," Mitch said as he added some pink flavoring to the lemonade. It was the way Katherine liked it.

Not sure what words she should use, Emma blurted out, "Do you ever feel like you're not good enough for Katherine?"

Mitch stopped fixing the refreshment and walked around the bar to sit next to Emma. He looked very serious.

He sat down and said, very seriously, "Every damn day."

Emma's eyes shot up to his and she asked, "Really?"

"I figure it this way," he said and smiled, "the day that I feel like I'm good enough or better is the day I'll forget that making that woman happy is the one job I hope I never quit or get fired from."

Listening, Emma nodded.

Mitch wasn't always comfortable expressing things but he cleared his throat and added, "She's the person who's having my children, the one that makes me smile, the one that makes me feel like I have a purpose, and the one who accepts me for all the things I am, good and bad."

Emma was speechless. Even though she'd only really known Mitch well for the last couple of years, she respected his opinion.

"Too mushy?" Mitch asked her.

Shaking her head no, Emma answered, "No, not at all."

Nodding, Mitch stood up and walked back around the counter. He poured two glasses of lemonade and handed one to Emma.

He raised his glass, "Here's to figuring it all out," he said.

Emma figured that Mitch had no idea what a mouthful he just said.

Eventually Emma went back into the room and, after a round of hugs and "I'm sorry", the four friends went back to talking about whatever they wanted.

The next morning Emma was up early and went for a run with Abi. They ran through a nearby park and were almost numb when they got back in. Early November in Virginia wasn't the best time to run outside.

Other than the biting wind, the weather was actually pretty nice. The sun shone brightly and everyone seemed to be in good spirits.

Emma and Abi arrived early to help both Eryn's and Katherine's mom with any final preparations.

Beverly Fredricks gave Eryn's friends a hug and gushed over them.

"You both look stunning," she said to them.

Abi sighed, and said, "Thanks, I'm trying to look good for the wedding."

Emma took that as her cue to find Katherine's mother and see if she needed help. The wedding plans weren't something Emma was particularly excited about.

Victoria Fredricks was standing near a table, staring at it intently.

"Did you need some help, Mrs. Fredricks?" Emma asked softly.

Jumping in surprise, Victoria turned to Katherine's friend, "Oh dear, no, I'm just looking at this table and wondering how to decorate it."

Not wanting to laugh and embarrass Katherine's mother, Emma merely said, "I'm here to help so, if you don't mind, I can offer some suggestions from other baby showers I've attended?"

Smiling, Victoria said, "That would be so helpful, Emma, thank you."

Emma nodded and got to work. It was nice to feel needed, even if it was just for decorating a table for a baby shower.

The shower went off without a hitch, although it was the largest baby shower Emma ever saw.

There were at least forty women there. No wonder they needed to have it in a banquet hall! Emma was in charge of getting the guests situated upon arrival and Abi was assigned to coordinate the games.

Both Mommies-to-Be were beaming and looked beautiful.

Emma stood on the outskirts of the crowd as gifts were opened. She stared in amazement at some of the gadgets people gave to Eryn and Katherine. Emma hadn't even known a lot of it existed before today.

She stared at the mounds of gifts that piled up and was trying to figure out how to get them back to Katherine and Mitch's place. How Eryn was going to get them all back to Hawaii was a thought she didn't even want to entertain.

The last gift was opened and the last guest was thanked about three hours later.

Emma plopped down on a chair next to Eryn's mom and sighed.

"My thoughts exactly," Beverly said with a smile.

Eryn absently rubbed her feet, "Thank you all for doing this, it was wonderful," she said with tears springing to her eyes.

Katherine stood up and slapped her hands together, "Well," she said, "we should probably call the men and have them pick us up."

Abi nodded, "Yes," she said excitedly, "Gav should be here by now."

Emma's eyes shot over to her friend's.

"He called earlier and said he wanted to see me," Abi said to Emma.

The women all ahhhhed but Emma was upset. She knew that, rationally, she shouldn't be. Abi would naturally want to see her fiancé. Even knowing that though, Emma felt kind of betrayed.

Not even twenty minutes later, the men arrived. They loaded up gifts and then everyone decided that they would meet up for dinner.

Emma was pretty sure she didn't want to be the only one there without a partner so she begged off, citing a headache.

Abi watched her friend and knew her excuse wasn't true.

Back at the hotel, Emma plopped down on the bed and sighed. Without thinking, she picked up the phone and called Braedon.

Chapter 26

Braedon was sitting on his back patio, trying to figure out if his neighbor was going to set the whole apartment building on fire, when his phone rang.

Distracted by his neighbor's pouring of copious amounts of lighter fluid onto an already large grill fire, he answered, "Hello," absently.

Emma thought he sounded off, "Hello, Braedon, its Emma," she said.

It took a second for Emma's words to permeate his mind. Once they did though, he was no longer thinking of his pyromaniac neighbor.

"Hey there," he said softly.

His voice sounded so good to Emma. Just hearing it made her feel better.

"What are you up to?" he asked, even though he knew what she was doing.

Both Mitch and Chase called him within the last week to see if he was coming to the baby shower weekend. They had some guy stuff planned and wanted to include him. He felt a little embarrassed by having to tell them that he wasn't coming.

To his surprise though, neither Mitch nor Chase seemed particularly concerned about it.

Emma mumbled, "Sitting here in a hotel room."

"Is the baby shower over with?" Braedon asked her.

'How did he know?' Emma asked herself then rolled her eyes. When she first asked him to go, she gave him all the dates.

Knowing that Braedon was waiting for her to answer, Emma said, "Yes, it was huge!"

Laughing, Braedon asked, "How big is huge?"

Spilling into a comical explanation of the event, Emma told him about all of it. She was smiling by the time she finished. It felt good to talk to him again.

Braedon could hear the change in her tone as she talked. She became more comfortable. He wondered if she realized that, when she was stressed, she inflected her words a specific way?

"What did you get them?" he asked when she quieted down.

Rolling her eyes, Emma answered, "Gift cards, what else?"

Laughing, Braedon should have known that Emma wouldn't want it to be complicated. She was, on a lot of levels, a no-nonsense woman.

"Good thinking," he said, smiling.

Knowing she needed to say something, Emma sat up a little straighter before asking him, "Are you there alone?"

Torn between being annoyed and flattered, Braedon sat down on the couch in the living room.

Answering her question with one of his own, Braedon asked, "Does it matter?"

That question was complicated in a ton of ways. Emma knew she was about to sacrifice some of her pride and she didn't like it one bit.

"What if I was to say yes?" she asked.

Dealing with Emma was a little like playing poker, Braedon decided. He needed to gauge the odds.

Smiling, he asked, "What if I was to say, 'What do you think?'"

Shaking her head, Emma asked back, "What if I was to say that I miss you?"

That, Braedon was not expecting. He anticipated that Emma would ride out however long it took for him to give in. The fact that she didn't made him wonder.

"I'd probably say that I miss you too," he answered.

Just hearing the words from Braedon, Emma felt a lot better. She knew that one conversation wasn't going to fix everything, but it was a step in the right direction.

Emma sighed, "Good."

They seemed to make an unspoken agreement to avoid the subject of their last phone call. Emma asked him about Jason and Kathy and he asked about her friends.

Before they hung up, Braedon asked, "So how is Mrs. Fredricks doing?"

Laughing, Emma knew he was talking about Eryn's mother who he monopolized on the dance floor at Mitch and Katherine's reception.

"She's very well, thank you," she said to him and added, "I'll pass on your wishes."

Smiling wide, Braedon added, "You do that."

They hung up a few minutes later with Emma feeling a lot better. She ordered some room service, figuring she deserved a little pampering, and then ordered a romantic comedy on the TV she'd been wanting to see. The whole time she was smiling and thinking about Braedon and wishing he was here with her.

Braedon hung up with Emma and shot his fist into the air. He was relieved she called him. He also knew it cost her emotionally to do so. Then he wondered if that was all she was willing to pay.

The plane ride back to California was easy; Emma passed most of the time with reading. She had some stuff to catch up on for work and answered emails while she waited at Dallas/Fort Worth for her layover. Being efficient was something Emma required of herself when it came to work.

Sitting on the plane to San Diego, she wondered what she would do about Braedon. She missed him that was for sure. They had talked twice while she was in Virginia but hadn't really made any plans for when she got back.

It was late in the evening when she arrived at the house.

After parking in the garage, Emma grabbed her bag and went inside. She pulled out the dirty clothes from her bag and tossed them into the washing machine before taking the bag upstairs to her room.

Emma made quick work of putting the rest of her things away and slipping on some sweat pants and a plain t-shirt. She was on her way downstairs when she heard her phone ringing. Picking it up from the kitchen counter, she smiled when she saw it was Braedon.

"Well, hello there," she said as she grabbed a soda from the refrigerator.

Braedon smiled at the sound of her voice and said, "You sound like you're home."

Sighing, Emma sat down in a chair and answered, "Just got here about fifteen minutes ago."

Sitting on his patio, Braedon was watching some of the guys in his apartment complex playing basketball. Sometimes he would be out there joining them but tonight he wanted to hear Emma's voice. If any of them knew that, he'd never hear the end of it.

"Are you tired?" he asked.

Emma leaned back against the soft fabric of the chair and absently rubbed the arm of it.

Smiling, she said, "Not really. I'd probably be awake enough for you to say......come over and make love to me."

Standing up, Braedon almost tripped over a plant in his hurried attempt to get inside and grab his car keys.

"Yes, ma'am," he answered quickly and was locking his apartment door.

Emma didn't even say good bye. She hung up and ran back upstairs to find something more suitable to wear.

Braedon was at her house inside of twenty-five minutes. It wouldn't have taken that long normally, but he was in a hurry and so everyone on the roads seemed to be against his getting to his destination.

Walking up to the front door, he thought that he should have brought something for her. Flowers, candy, something.

Emma opened the door just as Braedon was about to knock. She unceremoniously grabbed him and pulled him inside, her lips crushing against his.

If he wasn't so excited to see Emma, he would have slowed down. As soon as she kissed him, he was possessed by a want so deep down inside of him, he didn't know if it could ever be completely sated.

"I missed you," Emma said against his lips as they made their way through the entryway and to the stairs.

Braedon let his hands travel up and down Emma's body, he was kissing her and didn't feel like talking. He only wanted to explore every part of her.

At the bottom of the stairs, Braedon turned so he was leading her up to her room.

They were in her bedroom when he said, "I've missed you too."

'Funny,' Emma thought to herself, 'hearing those words is more arousing than anything else.'

Emma shut the door behind them to drown out the rest of the world, and pulled the tie from her bathrobe. She let the fabric fall to the floor around her feet. When she saw Braedon's reaction to her bedroom attire, she wanted to laugh.

Braedon was turning around to pull Emma to him when she dropped her bathrobe.

All the thoughts in his head were sucked out. She stood there, in a black lace teddy, complete with garter belt and stockings.

"Uh," Braedon managed to murmur.

Smiling, Emma walked the few steps to where he was, "That's what I was hoping for."

He brought his hands up to cup Emma's face and looked into her eyes. They reflected everything Braedon wanted to see in them; want, need, and…..maybe something deeper.

Being kissed by Braedon was amazing! Emma watched his eyes drift shut as his lips came down to join with hers. For some inexplicable reason, she kept hers slightly open, wanting to see him.

Even with his eyes closed, the dim light, and their faces so close, he was just.....beautiful.

Turning them around, Emma pulled back just enough to lead him over to the bed. She didn't want to think too deeply about all of this now; she wanted him.

Emma laid on the bed and held her legs up to his chest. She watched as he, very gently, undid the garters on her thighs and slowly peeled the stockings down her legs. Once he removed them, he kissed first on one foot then the other, his hands massaging the arches of her feet at the same time.

How could something so simple feel so decadent? Emma wanted to purr from the sensations running through her.

Braedon lowered her legs so they were on each side of him. He stood there, at the edge of the bed, and pulled off his shirt. Next were his shoes. Finally he undid the fly of his jeans and pushed them down.

There was no hiding his reaction to Emma. Not that he wanted to. She should know what she did to him.

Watching Braedon remove his clothes and laying there watching his arousal was making Emma hotter by the second. Goosebumps ran up her body in anticipation of his touch.

She reached out and silently asked him to join her. He crawled onto the bed, resting his hips between hers. Her lace panties were the only barrier between them now.

Kissing her again, deeply, Braedon was swallowed up into the swell of chemistry between them. He was pretty sure they could light up the city of San Diego with the electricity humming between them.

Emma arched in an effort to get closer. They were touching each other and his kisses were sending her higher and higher into the universe of incoherent thought. Her body was wound tightly and the only release would be given by Braedon.

Braedon ran his hands down Emma's sides. He could feel her heat against his shaft. He moaned when she shifted and he knew if he didn't take control now, he would tumble over the edge of this crazy mountain.

Reaching down, Braedon ran his fingers over the flimsy lace panties she wore before catching the edge and sliding his fingers beneath the fabric to touch her soft, swelling sex.

"Ahhhh," Emma hissed and arched her back again.

Smiling, Braedon dipped his finger into her deeper and started massaging her swollen nub.

He looked down at her wild eyes and knew he loved her, "That's right, Emma," he whispered, "let me feel you."

There was no way Emma could stop the onslaught of crazy sensations that were pouring over her. Every time his fingers moved, she was driven up a little higher to the precipice her body screamed for.

Knowing Emma was close drove Braedon further into madness. He pulled his fingers out of Emma just enough to move the fabric aside and allow his hard member to enter her.

Emma arched one last time as Braedon entered her. The orgasm hit her body with such force that she literally saw stars as her eyes clenched in reaction.

"Yes," Braedon whispered in Emma's ear.

He softly brushed her hair with his fingertips as she drifted back down to reality.

Opening her eyes, Emma smiled and said, "Your turn."

Braedon was sure that she meant it.

Chapter 27

Two weeks after returning from Virginia, Emma sat in her boss's office listening to a preliminary meeting about holiday hours for the airfield.

She took notes, commented on certain things, and asked appropriate questions but her mind wasn't 100% present in the meeting.

Frustrated because her mind was wandering…..again, Emma frowned.

She always prided herself on being in the thick of it at work. Being able to put out any potential work-related "fires" was part of her job and she couldn't even get through one stinking meeting.

Her boss, thankfully, ended the meeting and Emma went back to her own office to work. It just so happened that her office was on the end of the building that faced Crash Crew. She never noticed that before. AND, she never noticed that if she stood up and walked to the window, that she could look into the stairway of that building.

A few days earlier she noticed it and called Braedon on his cell. He picked up and she told him to go to that very same stairway. After he did, they sat on the phone for a good twenty minutes and looked at one another as they talked.

This was not the behavior of a Senior Staff NCO in the Marine Corps. This was not the behavior of a level headed woman who always made her work the priority in her life.

Maybe that was it.

Emma pushed her chair back from the desk so she could prop her boots on the top of it. Until recently, she would've considered such an action as unprofessional. What was going on here?

Her phone rang and brought her back to reality.

"Master Gunnery Sgt. Cantrell," she answered formally.

There was a pause before she heard, "Boy, you sound like you're serious," from Abi.

Happy for the distraction, Emma brought her boots back to the ground and smiled.

"I'm just frustrated," she answered.

Smiling, Abi asked, "Work?"

Emma sighed, "Yes."

Abi didn't believe her for one nano second.

"Well," Abi started, "I've been talking to Gav-"

Emma interrupted by saying, "That's a good thing since you're marrying him."

Danette Fogarty

Abi rolled her eyes and said, "Funny," in a dry voice. "Anyway," she added, "we've decided to move up the wedding."

Sitting up straighter, Emma was intrigued.

"May I ask why?" Emma asked.

Blushing, Abi played with her engagement ring as she sat in her room. She had talked to Gav the night before and it was too late to call anyone else so she waited until the morning to let her friends in on the change of plans.

Clearing her throat, Abi said, "I want to be married, I want him here, I want us to start out life together," her voice rushed because of excitement.

Emma rolled her eyes, too a breath, then asked, "Is it that difficult to be engaged?"

"It's difficult to be away from Gav," Abi sighed, "It's not like he can't move here now but we really want to be married."

Even though Emma listened, she wasn't sure she understood the issue here. Of course, the choice was Abi's and Gav's, not hers. She was there to support of her friends.

Sighing, Emma asked, "When and where?" and picked up her pen.

The afternoon went smoothly after the call from Abi and Emma got home in a reasonable amount of time. There was really no reason that she should be testy or restless, and yet, she was.

She got dressed and went downstairs to take out her aggressions on the punching bag in the garage.

Twenty minutes of beating the crap out of an inanimate object did wonders for one's nerves.

Emma came back inside and turned on her CD player, the sound of country music filling the house.

She didn't understand why people labelled the music as sad and sappy. The current CD was upbeat and made her feel happy. Personally, she felt that the genre was genuinely kind and true to life.

The whole house was wired for sound so the music followed her upstairs as she stripped out of her workout gear.

Showering was a lot more fun to do to a soundtrack. Emma sung along with some of the songs she knew really well and didn't massacre with her lack of musical ability.

She was stepping out of the shower when her phone went off.

Wrapping herself into a towel, Emma went over and saw it was her father.

"Dad," she answered brightly.

Her father was her rock. He supported her no matter what and encouraged her during her career. She always felt so guilty about being the one who drove her mother away from him. He always told her it wasn't her fault but that didn't stop Emma from holding onto the burden.

Smiling, Tim Cantrell said, "Hello there, daughter."

Emma couldn't help but smile at the quirky greeting. That was her dad.

"What's up?" Emma asked as she towel-dried her hair.

Tim was nervous. He knew he shouldn't be, but he was. It took a minute for him to say the words.

"Uh," he started, "you know I've been in contact with your mom."

Emma stopped and closed her eyes in the hopes of keeping tears from falling.

She answered, "Yes," softly.

Tim heard his daughter's reluctance. Lord knew he'd had his fair share of it himself. When Cynthia left, he felt gutted emotionally and only managed to pull himself together enough for his daughters. After they were grown and gone, he concentrated on his work. It helped keep the pain out. Emma was the most like him and he knew she would be the hardest sell on the situation with her mother.

He kept his tone even as he spoke, "Well, I've asked her to come home."

Even though Emma knew this was what was going to happen, it was still like a punch to her gut. She knew her mother was sorry and was trying to mend the hurt between them. But did she deserve to have a life with the man she broke so many years ago? 'It's not your call,' her conscience called out.

"Okay," Emma answered.

Tim knew she would be accepting but only for his sake. He wanted his daughters to heal too. The others were already working on repairing their relationships with their mother and he knew Emma would be the toughest.

Clearing his throat, Tim asked, "Would you be willing to come home for Thanksgiving?"

After the earlier meeting, Emma knew she could probably get away with taking the weekend off but she didn't want to. Not yet.

"I uh," she said slowly, "have duty so I can't."

Tim knew she wasn't being honest. Another thing he passed on to his eldest daughter was her inability to lie convincingly.

Danette Fogarty

"I see," he answered, then added, "if you change your mind though, we'd love to see you."

Emma nodded and said, "You got it."

Knowing their talk was over, Tim said, "Okay….well, I'm going to go. I love you."

She did know that her dad loved her, he was never one to deny her that.

"Dad," she said quickly before he disconnected, "I'm happy if you're happy."

Tim knew she meant that but it was difficult for her. He was proud of the woman she had become. He wanted her to find happiness.

He spoke softly, "Thank you, Emma, I'll talk to you soon."

Emma hadn't even disconnected the call before the tears streamed down her cheeks.

She sat on her bed and cried like a little girl, balled up as if putting up a wall to keep the world out.

Braedon knocked and walked in. Since Emma came back from Virginia, he'd come over three nights a week. It was sort of a thing they came up with so they each kept their own stuff on track. He didn't have much to say about it, it was Emma's deal but he accepted it because it was the only way to keep her in his life for right now.

He heard a noise from upstairs and thought maybe she was cleaning or something.

As he reached the top of the stairs, he could hear the distinct sounds of crying and rushed into her room. He stopped in his tracks when he saw her.

She looked like a little girl, curled up and sobbing. It broke his heart and he quietly made his way across the room and gently laid his hand on Emma's shoulder.

"Baby," he whispered, "what is it?"

Emma wasn't even surprised that she hadn't heard Braedon come inside. She was wallowing her own pain and needed some relief. Looking up, she saw the worry in his eyes and it was almost her undoing.

She managed, somehow, to sit up.

Braedon sat beside her and rubbed her arm before asking, "What's going on?"

His voice was soft and felt soothing to Emma's nerves. She couldn't voice what was wrong, so she moved over until she was encircled in his arms. They were strong and protected her from all of the other bullshit that was swimming around in her brain.

Braedon held her. After a few minutes, he shifted so they were seated against the headboard of her bed, Emma spread out beside him but still in his arms.

He didn't ask anything again, deciding that she would tell him when she was ready.

After an hour, Emma finally calmed down. Her breathing returned to normal and she absently played with a button on the front of Braedon's shirt. Her thoughts were running through her mind like a ticker tape, repeating the hurtful things her mother did.

The sun was setting, casting shadows inside her bedroom. Braedon moved so he could see her face.

"Are you going to tell me?" he asked her softly.

Shrugging her shoulders, Emma asked, "Do I have to?"

For some reason he couldn't explain, anger filled his mind. What the hell kind of question was that? Didn't she know that she needed to share with him if they were going to be in a relationship?

He tried to keep his emotions in check and nodded yes.

Emma mentally geared up for her explanation. Saying the words out loud gave them life and she so did not want to do that.

Looking at him, she almost broke down again. She did not make a habit of bearing things to people, most especially men and Braedon would be the first.

"My mother used to parade me around to beauty pageants when I was a kid," she started, then using her hands to create circles, she added, "not like little ones, she wanted the whole thing, like Miss America or Miss Universe."

Braedon nodded but didn't comment.

Looking up at the ceiling, Emma tried to organize her words.

She blew out a breath and said, "Okay, so I didn't want to do it anymore, right?" She shook her hands as if to shake off the memories before saying, "I wanted to get away as far and as fast as possible, so I joined the Corps."

He knew there was a point, but didn't have it quite yet.

"Then my mom did something I still, to this day, DO NOT understand. She just left." As the words left her mouth, the tears started down her cheeks.

Cocking his head, Braedon asked, "What do you mean left?"

Looking frustrated, Emma said, "You know, packed her clothes, hopped in the car, and said adios to her husband and four," she put up four fingers for effect, "daughters."

The situation was starting to clear but Braedon still had questions.

He asked, "Did she come back?"

"No," Emma snapped but added, "That is, not until now." She took a breath, "NOW she just wants to go back to how it was, like a no harm, no foul thing."

Knowing that any rejection could hurt, especially as a child, he wanted to make sure he understood the situation. It might give him some insight on Emma's reaction.

Cupping her chin, Braedon wanted her to look at him when he asked, "You don't want to forgive her but your family, your father, does?"

Emma was not able to answer, she merely nodded.

Braedon remembered, all too well, how lost he was when his mom remarried and had more kids. She never left him and Jason though and they'd long since resolved any issues. It didn't take a PhD to figure out Emma never resolved hers. It went a long way in understanding why she was so control driven.

He also knew that there was absolutely nothing he could say to her to heal this part of her heart. His biggest fear was that it was too broken for her to let him in.

Suddenly, Braedon was really pissed at Emma's mother. It wasn't rational but, then again, love never was.

Chapter 28

The week after Emma's meltdown was Thanksgiving. Her father and sisters called her almost every day asking her to come be with them but she couldn't. And she wouldn't be the reason that they didn't have a nice holiday. So she stayed at her house and sulked most evenings.

Eryn called her and tried to pump information but Emma shut down. The only time she even spoke in full sentences was at work because she had to.

Braedon held her until she fell asleep that night, then left to go home. He left a note saying he would call her and he did, but she didn't answer.

She was embarrassed about being so weak in front of him and she was completely afraid he'd agree with her family about her going home and mending fences.

Sitting on the sofa, a bowl of uneaten popcorn next to her, Emma zoned out while the television droned on. She jumped when there was a knock at the door.

"If that is some salesperson I will scream," she mumbled as she climbed off the couch and trudged toward the front door.

She couldn't make out who was at the door through the peephole so she opened it slightly, keeping the chain lock engaged in case it was some serial killer.

"Emma Cantrell!" Eryn Johnson yelled, "You open this door right now or we're busting it open, I swear!"

Frowning, Emma closed the door, disengaged the lock and swung it open.

There, on her doorstep, were a very pregnant Eryn, a very stubborn looking Abi, and another very pregnant but sympathetic looking Katherine.

Seeing the three of them there, Emma started laughing and crying at the same time.

"It's worse than we thought," Abi said dryly, "she can't figure out if she's happy we're here or depressed."

They all came inside and gave Emma a group hug.

Feeling them around her, Emma felt better. Like her feet were finding some solid ground after a week of being in quicksand.

Katherine kissed her cheek and said, "I think she's glad."

They all laughed.

Emma release them and was glad her house wasn't messy. She started to walk into the kitchen but stopped and faced them all.

"What are you doing here?" she asked while putting her hands on her hips.

"Funny story," Eryn started, "Chase and I were considering coming stateside for the big Turkey day celebrations so we called Gav and Katherine and Mitch and told them to get their asses to the West Coast and meet us half way."

If Emma wasn't so desperate to have the three of them here, she would've called Eryn out for the lie she just told. Inside, she knew that Braedon had something to do with this, she just wasn't sure what.

The four of them sat at the kitchen bar and talked about the big Thanksgiving dinner the guys were cooking for the women.

It was easy to forget her personal crap when she was around Eryn, Abi, and Katherine. They made her *want* to laugh when an hour ago she was sure she'd never laugh again. Just their presence made her feel so loved, it was impossible to let the insecurities in.

They were laughing about something one of the guys at Eryn and Abi's work tried to pull when Emma got up to get out a soda.

"Are you guys going to tell me why you're really here?" she asked them quietly.

Eryn scooted off the barstool she was sitting on and came over to Emma.

She kissed Emma's cheek and asked, "How long have we been friends?"

Emma looked at Eryn and tried to hold back her emotions.

Abi and Katherine came over to them and they all stood in a circle.

"We would never," Eryn said sternly, "let you hurt and not come to help you heal."

Katherine spoke up and said, "I'm the newest member of this little gang and I don't think I could survive without all of you." She smiled and added, "Eryn may be my cousin, but all of you are my sisters."

Tears fell down Emma's cheeks and this time they were tears of happiness. She made a mental note to thank Braedon for getting them here.

The next day was Thanksgiving and, Emma was informed the night before that, the meal was being prepared at her house since she had quote, "the only place big enough."

She was up at just after 6am cleaning. She didn't want to have company and the house look awful.

An hour later, she was somewhat satisfied with her efforts when there was a knock at the door.

Looking through the peephole, her eyes widened in shock.

Opening the door, she found Chase, Mitch, Gav, Dave, Jason, and Braedon all standing there, loaded down with bags.

"Are you going to let us in or are we going to cook a turkey on your front lawn?" Chase asked loudly.

Laughing, Emma stepped aside and let the group enter.

She gave all of them kisses on the cheeks as they entered.

Braedon was the last one and after she gave him a kiss he turned and said, "I'll expect a better one a little later."

Emma was blown away with how the comment made her skin tingle. She looked at him, again, like he was a puzzle.

The guys went into the kitchen and took over. Emma was "ordered" to go get ready since the girls would be coming over soon.

She went upstairs and laughed at the bickering that had already commenced over which pan to use for what or how to make stuffing versus dressing.

Emma was ready just in time to get the door for the girls. They came in and hugged her tightly. Abi offered up a couple of bottles of wine.

"Even if the pregnant ones can't indulge, we'll drink their share," she said with a big smile.

Eryn stuck her tongue out at her friend and responded, "Only a little more than two more months and this one is coming," as she rubbed her rounded belly.

Emma shook her head and looked at Abi before asking, "How did you get them to agree to be bridesmaids in your wedding when they'll have to rent tents for their bodies?"

The question got her a pillow to the face and nasty glares.

Chase came into the room carrying Emma's phone.

"Em," he said, as he handed it to her, "phone call."

Still laughing about her comment, Emma answered, "Hello," with a smile on her face.

Tim Cantrell was relieved to hear noise around his daughter, "Emma," he said.

"Dad?" Emma asked and gave the girls a look before walking outside to listen privately.

Smiling, Tim commented, "I see you're with friends today."

Nodding, Emma replied, "Yes, they sort of showed up."

"I'm glad," Tim said.

Knowing her father, Emma asked, "Dad, why are you calling?"

'Yep,' Tim thought to himself, 'she's just like me.'

He nodded to his wife and spoke into the phone, "I just wanted to say that we understand why you couldn't come home now and we'll wait until you're ready."

Tears welled up in her eyes but Emma held them in.

"Thanks," she said, and added, "Dad, please tell Mom and the girls Happy Thanksgiving from me."

Tim's voice cracked as he answered, "Will do."

Her father hung up and Emma disconnected the line and slipped her phone into her pocket. She turned around to find Braedon standing by the front door. He must have come outside during her call.

"I suppose," Emma started as she walked over to him, "I owe you a pretty big thank you."

Braedon was happy to be with her and see her smile. If calling all over the place to get reinforcements did the trick, then it was worth it.

He tapped her nose with a finger before answering, "I'll have to think of something appropriate for you to do for me."

Emma kissed him quickly then went back inside. She loved a challenge!

Thanksgiving dinner was loud and the best time Emma could remember having over the holiday. They put up card tables on either side of Emma's dining table so everyone could fit.

The men served the meal with a flourish and, to the women's delight and relief, no bloodshed ensued during the preparation. Not to mention, the food looked fantastic.

Everyone was seated when Mitch stood up to say, "I think I'm the oldest so I think I should say the Blessing and toast."

There were comments shouted and noises made when the doorbell sounded. Frowning, Emma got up to answer it with Braedon right behind her.

She opened the door to find Kathy, the bartender from Bullz, standing there with a pie.

"Happy Thanksgiving," Kathy said nervously.

Emma smiled and invited her inside. Braedon took her coat and they directed her into the dining room.

"Did you invite her?" Emma asked Braedon.

He shook his head no but said, "I think Jason did." Then he added, "About damn time too."

Not sure what that meant, Emma decided to let it go and get back to the table.

Jason got another chair for Kathy while Chase got a place setting and everyone settled down once again.

Mitch stood and announced, "As I was saying….."

Everyone looked at him.

"This year has been a wonderful blessing for us as individuals and as a group," he started, "but I cannot think of another group of friends I'd rather celebrate with."

Chase said, "Here, here."

Mitch continued, "We ask for blessings for safe travels, for new families, for old friends, and most especially…… that Dave and Chase didn't overcook this turkey as I suspect they did. Amen."

Laughter erupted from the group and everyone started digging in.

Chapter 29

After Thanksgiving, Emma's spirits lifted and she seemed able to start reconciling some very old feelings. She called both of her parents to talk to them and promised to try harder to get their family back together.

During their visit, Abi, Eryn, and Katherine dragged her to a seamstress Katherine knew in San Diego to be fitted for bridesmaid dresses for Abi and Gav's wedding in January.

"Who gets married in January?" Emma asked Abi sarcastically.

Abi just smiled sweetly and said, "Me!"

Emma was walking into work the following week smiling, and thinking of Abi's silly smile. She was happy for Abi and knew she deserved to be happy. And if the sharp-dressed Russian did that for her, then he must be good people too.

"Hey, Master Guns," one of the Corporals who worked with her said as he passed.

Emma smiled and said, "Good morning," before making her way toward her office.

She felt…..almost light. It was a sunny and somewhat cool day. Her friends were doing well and she had……Braedon.

She'd just sat down when a co-worker came into her office.

It was a Staff Sgt. who worked in a different section of Airfield Operations but had a bit of interaction with Emma from time to time.

"Master Guns," Staff Sgt. Fellings said, as she knocked on Emma's office door.

Emma motioned her inside and smiled before asking, "What can I do for you today, Staff Sgt.?"

Sitting down, Staff Sgt. Fellings looked nervous. "Uh, I wanted to ask you a question."

Intrigued, Emma said, "Okayyyy," she asked, "What is it?"

Sitting forward, Staff Sgt. Fellings quietly asked Emma, "Who is it?"

Not understanding, Emma leaned forward and asked back, "Who is what?"

Looking at the door, as if she were paranoid, the Staff Sgt. said, "Who is the guy you're in love with?" She added, "The pool is up to about a thousand dollars and I could really use the money."

Emma's stomach felt like it was just drop kicked across the airfield. The Staff Sgt.'s words made her blood run cold and anger light up quicker than an engine of an F-18 fighter jet.

Calmly, Emma stood up and walked around her desk. She stood in front of the Staff Sgt. with her hands clasped together because if she didn't she was afraid that she would pummel the woman.

"Up," Emma managed to say with only a slight edge of anger.

The Staff Sgt. stood quickly, getting the drift right away, and said, "I'm so sorry, I thought you knew."

Emma looked at the woman and said, "If you know what is good for your career and the career of those who have nothing better to do than bet on the lives of others," she smiled but there was no warmth in it. "I suggest you disband this "bet" as soon as possible."

Nodding, the woman left the office quickly, completely embarrassed.

Emma closed her office door and didn't speak to anyone for the rest of the day.

Braedon came into Crash Crew and smiled at the guys from the crews as they were cleaning the trucks.

He felt like Thanksgiving was a turning point for Emma. She seemed more open to her parents and, he hoped, to the feelings between her and him. Even though they hadn't slept together since, Braedon felt like they were building up their friendship and that was just as important as the sex. Maybe not quite as much fun, he admitted, but necessary.

Walking down the hall, he happened to pass by the NCOIC's office and heard a couple of the guys in there talking.

It was normal and he would have kept on walking but the words, "Master Guns at Air Ops," tripped an invisible switch in his head.

He backtracked and popped his head inside to ask, "Hey guys, what's up?"

Staff Sgt. Carson said, "Hey Master Sgt., do you want in on a bet?"

Braedon entered the room and said, "Maybe," before asking, "what's the bet?"

Gunny Roberts laughed and said, "You know that ice queen Master Guns over at Air Ops? Well, rumor is she's got someone who's thawing her out pretty good." He laughed and said, "They've got a grand riding on who it is."

Knowing that something wasn't right didn't necessarily prevent someone from doing it anyway.

Braedon knew, if he struck a co-worker, he could be punished, even arrested, but it didn't matter. This clown was talking about Emma and Braedon wouldn't stand for it.

Before Gunny Roberts knew what happened, Braedon pulled him out of the chair he was sitting in and had him up against the wall.

"Last time I checked, Gunnery Sgt.," Braedon said through gritted teeth, "Marines are expected to act like gentlemen."

He let go of the Gunnery Sgt. and walked out of the office to head straight for the OIC's office and explain.

When Braedon left for the day, he was somewhat relieved he didn't hit the other jackass and even more relieved that his boss was fair and gave him the benefit of the doubt. Higher ranks were expected to set the examples, not act like hormone jacked adolescents.

Of course, none of that mattered right now. What he was really worried about was what Emma knew. If she didn't know about the bet, it was only a matter of time. And if she did find out about it, heaven help the person who told her.

He didn't see her car as he left work so he figured she was gone for the day. Not wanting to waste any time, he got into his car and headed for her place.

Emma asked to leave work a little early, citing a headache. Her boss okayed it but she was pretty sure he knew that she knew about that stupid bet.

Just thinking about it made her want to vomit.

She spent her whole career trying to be an equal to the men and women she worked with, to prove herself as a capable person in her chosen profession. Time and time again, she was judged by her appearance so she got into the habit of being distant. It wasn't that she didn't like people, it was that she wanted to be taken seriously.

This wasn't the first time she was the butt of a joke; you couldn't spend eighteen years in the Corps, or any job for that matter, without having the occasional jerk or bully. But she had always dealt with it professionally.

So now, look what it got her? They looked at her differently because maybe she smiled more or was just a little less abrasive.

To her way of thinking, if people could joke and spend that much money on who she was dating, then they didn't take her seriously at all.

If this is what having a relationship meant, then what was the point?   If sharing meant opening yourself to hurt, then why do it?

By the time she arrived at home, her mind was made up. This thing with Braedon had to stop now. She wouldn't let him be thrown into this circus. He was a nice guy and, even if they had a great chemistry, he didn't need this extra crap added on. Eventually he'd resent her anyway and leave so why not save him the trouble now?

Exhausted from her tumultuous thoughts, Emma went upstairs and fell onto her bed. She was asleep within minutes.

She woke up to pounding on her door followed by her doorbell. Getting up, she padded down the stairs and to the door. She opened it up before looking because she knew it was Braedon.

"Come in," she said and stepped aside so he could enter.

It didn't escape Braedon's notice that she didn't hug or kiss him when he came in. He knew she knew about that damn bet.

He stopped just past her and waited for her to shut the door before saying, "I guess you've heard."

Emma nodded and led the way into the kitchen.

"Are you okay?" Braedon asked and walked over to hold her.

Emma stepped away from him.

Braedon knew what she was going to do before she even spoke. His gut was on fire, his chest wanted to explode, and he knew she was going to break his heart.

Emma took a deep breath and said, "I don't want you wrapped up in this bullshit."

His anger getting more intense by the second, he snapped, "Do you think I give a damn about it?"

Knowing his anger would make it easier, Emma started right in, "I worked my ass off my whole career!" she shouted at him.

"And I haven't?" he shot back.

Nodding, Emma tried to calm down, "I know you have but you're not a woman."

Shaking his head, Braedon responded, "I am most certainly not and I can understand why there are some dumbasses who made you feel that way. But Emma," he calmed his tone before saying, "that's not me."

Emma pushed him away with her hands. She couldn't think clearly when he was that close and she needed to think clearly right now.

"All I know is," she tried to calm herself before saying, "I won't have some damn bet make a laughing stock out of me, Braedon."

He turned to go but stopped just before he reached the doorway to the living room and asked, "That's just code for I don't want to see you anymore. Isn't it, Emma?"

The fact that Emma just stood there and didn't say anything confirmed that they both knew she meant yes.

Braedon nodded in defeat and walked out of Emma's house.

Hours later, Emma laid in her bed and replayed their conversation over and over in her mind. The only sound she couldn't get out of her head was the soft click of the front door latch as he left.

The next morning, Emma got up and ready for work and was even there a little early.

She walked into the building and was greeted by the same Corporal from the day before. This time his greeting was only answered with a curt nod.

The Corporal walked down the hall and shook his head.

Emma was at her desk trying to finish some paperwork before lunch when her phone rang.

"Master Gunnery Sgt. Cantrell, how may I help you?" she said in a no nonsense tone.

Eryn just got into work at KBay and read her emails when she figured she better give Emma a call. Not knowing how to ask the question without pissing off her friend, Eryn figured she should just dive right in.

Eryn blew out a breath, "Hello there, friend, I see you've broken another heart."

The comment floored Emma. She wasn't expecting those words from Eryn.

"Excuse me?" she asked loudly.

Shaking her head, Eryn said, "Don't 'excuse me', Emma, you broke up with him!"

The words were loud and surprised both of them. They never spoke to one another like this.

Getting up to close the door, Emma made sure no one was directly outside her office, closed it, and then replied in a sarcastic tone, "What the hell does it matter? It seems like you think this is some sort of pattern!"

Eryn tried to calm down. She didn't mean her words to sound so awful.

"I'm sorry," she said to Emma, and dropped her volume.

Tears sprang to Emma's eyes. It felt like her tidy little world was systematically coming unglued.

Sitting back down, Emma asked, "What did you hear?"

Abi knocked and entered Eryn's office. Eryn handed her an email and she sat on the sofa as she read it. After looking over it, she looked up at Eryn with worry in her eyes.

"I got an email this morning," Eryn said as she took the page back from Abi, "and it says that Master Sgt. Richards is inquiring about openings elsewhere."

Emma's head snapped up and she asked, "Can he do that?"

Frowning, Eryn said, "He can if there's a billet available. With his promotion he can go into a higher position."

"Shit!" Emma said and slammed her fist down on the desk.

Eryn smiled for the first time and responded with, "I agree."

Abi motioned for the phone so Eryn handed it to her.

"What happened?" Abi asked.

Emma told them about the bet and how she wouldn't let something so petty affect her career. She was embarrassed about it and how a Staff Sgt. came in and asked her for inside information because she needed the money.

Abi shook her head and said, "Jackass!"

Emma wasn't sure exactly who Abi was referring to, but it pretty much described all parties involved so she let it go.

Holding up her hand to ask Eryn to wait a moment before talking, Abi asked, "Are you going to let him go?"

Sighing, Emma leaned back and answered, "I don't think I have much of a choice."

Chapter 30

December swept into San Diego with a fury and, normally, Emma would've hated the foul weather but now she relished it. It matched her mood perfectly.

Work was slow this time of year, mainly the squadrons operated with lower staffing numbers since Marines wanted to go home to see their families around the holidays.

Emma's parents asked her several times to come home for Christmas but she told them she was using up her leave for Abi's wedding. They accepted it and Emma felt a little guilty since it wasn't the whole truth.

In mid-December, Emma was asked to pick up the bridesmaid dresses from the seamstress they saw over Thanksgiving weekend.

Emma drove to the shop and waited patiently for the owner to come out.

"Hello there, can I help you?" the woman asked.

Smiling, Emma stood and said, "I'm here for the dresses for the Rochelle wedding."

The woman looked through her files and frowned.

Emma remembered that Katherine brought them in so she added, "They may be under Fredricks or Frinnel."

Smiling, the woman pulled the card out, looked it over and said, "Oh you're Katherine's friend and this is for the wedding in New York, right?"

Nodding, Emma waited for the woman to go behind a curtain, and she sat down.

A few minutes later, the woman and the dresses came back out. She pulled one of them out and asked Emma, "Are you going to try yours on?"

Not expecting to do that, Emma shook her head and said, "I don't think so."

Smiling the woman pursed her lips like a school teacher about to reprimand a student and said, "You'll try it on for my benefit, I'm sure. I'd hate for it not to fit and have Katherine give me that steely eyed look she's known for."

Coughing, in order to keep from laughing, Emma just nodded and followed the lady to the back. It was hard to think of Katherine and "steely eyed" in the same sentence.

"Now," the woman directed, "You remove your bra since there's one built in and try this on. I'll zip it when you come out."

Nodding, Emma waited for her to close the door to the dressing room and stripped down.

She opened the bag and almost gasped.

The dress was not just a dress…..it was a work of art!

Emma pulled the garment out of the bag and loved the way the fabric felt on her skin. It was done in a deep red with sequins that made up an empire waist with a soft velvet on the top and a chiffon overlay across the skirt. Emma pulled it on and instantly felt gorgeous.

She let her hair down and it fell, in soft waves, over the fabric. The softness of her light brown hair against the deep colored dress gave Emma a fairy-like appearance.

When she came out of the dressing room, the lady who helped her gasped and called for someone named Bonnie.

A couple of seconds later, another woman showed up. Emma assumed this was Bonnie and was about to laugh until she saw their faces.

"Oh my," Bonnie said and put her hand to her throat, "I wouldn't have expected it, Gretchen."

Emma looked from Bonnie to Gretchen and wondered if she had damaged the dress in some way. She was a little relieved that she now knew the owner's name and wouldn't feel silly.

Gretchen went behind Emma and zipped up the dress. She frowned when she came around to the front and pointed at Emma.

"You've lost weight," she said accusingly.

Emma blushed, "I'll eat a little more okay," she answered, not wanting to tick off this Gretchen woman.

Shaking her head, Gretchen said, "You'd better."

Emma's eyes met up with Bonnie's and she couldn't understand what the lady was gawking at until Gretchen took her by the shoulders and turned her around so she was facing a three way mirror.

Seeing the dress on and zipped gave it even more of a magical appearance.

Whispering, "Good job, Katherine," Emma turned this way and that way to see how it looked.

The back of the dress had a diamond shaped cut out to give the appearance of sexy without seeming gaudy. The chiffon overlay had crystals in it so they sparkled in the light as Emma moved. There were crystals done at the cuffs as well which reminded Emma of a medieval design.

She stayed in the dress a good fifteen minutes before deciding she couldn't live in the thing until New Year's.

Gretchen put it back into the bag and reminded Emma to eat before she left the shop.

Emma dialed Katherine's number in Virginia as she was leaving the shop. She carefully hung the dresses in the back seat of her car as the phone rang.

Katherine picked up on the fourth ring and said, "Katherine Frinnel."

Smiling, Emma thought how lucky Katherine was that her married name wasn't that different than her maiden name.

"Oh my gosh," Emma said into the phone.

Thinking there was something wrong, Katherine dropped the fabric swatches she was studying and said, "Emma? What's wrong? Did she mess up the dresses?"

Emma got into her car and started it up but didn't put it into drive because she was on the phone. She looked in the rearview mirror and the dresses took of her entire view.

"NO!" Emma said emphatically, "She did an amazing job. YOU did an amazing job!"

Settling down from her scare, Katherine smiled. She never tired of someone thinking one of her designs was beautiful. That was what a designer strived for on a daily basis.

Sighing, Katherine answered, "Oh good, you had me worried."

"Sorry," Emma said, "but they are breathtaking."

Chuckling, Katherine sat down at her desk. The baby made her tire more easily and she didn't know how much longer she would be able to work full time.

Snapping back to the phone conversation, Katherine asked, "So is Braedon coming with you to the wedding?"

Emma's previous elation was sucked out of her at the mention of Braedon's name. He was the one thing that she and Eryn argued about. He was the thing that tore up her professional life. But he was also the one person she dreamed about every single night and wished she could see.

"Katherine," Emma started, but Katherine interrupted her.

Waving to her assistant for some privacy, Katherine said, "Wait, before you get into all the reasons why he's not coming along, can you tell me that you don't think about him?"

Knowing she needed to be honest with her friend, Emma answered, "No, I can't say that."

"Okay," Katherine said and dropped the subject.

They hung up a short time later with Emma wondering what exactly the point of the conversation was.

Christmas was coming up so the day after Emma picked up the dresses, she requested off to do some shopping for gifts. She figured it would be easier to do on a weekday; less people.

When she got to the mall in Escondido, she realized no one else got the memo that said stay away from the mall. It was packed.

By the time Emma found a parking space and made her way inside, she was ready to go home and nap.

Only her stubborn pride kept her going and she pulled out her list of people and their intended gifts.

Emma was a planner by nature and purchasing Christmas gifts was in no way different than anything else. She had a list of people and spent weeknights and weekends researching online to find the perfect gift.

She also refused to purchase gifts online, preferring to pick it out and physically purchase it in person.

An hour into the, what she could only describe as, the ordeal, Emma was running short on patience.

The crowds were acceptable but, between the stressed out store clerks and screaming toddlers, she was spent. Hoping to find a small bit of respite, she made her way to the food court and was standing in line when she heard someone calling her name.

Looking around, she didn't see anyone she recognized until her name was said again. Her eyes widened when she realized it was Kathy, the bartender from Bullz, calling her. And to top that, Braedon's brother Jason, was with her. And, if Emma's radar was still working, they looked awful chummy as they walked toward her.

"Hey," she said to Kathy and hugged her.

Seeing Jason was a little more difficult for Emma because he looked like Braedon. Not a lot but enough to make Emma's chest hurt.

She leaned over and kissed Jason on the cheek and said, "Are you both putting yourself through the torturous task of Christmas shopping?"

Kathy nodded, "We figured we'd carpool and be shopping buddies," she said brightly.

If Emma saw the look they shot one another, shopping wasn't the only thing they were buddies at. She was glad for them.

The three of them stood there and chatted for a few minutes while Emma waited in line to order her food. The conversation was light but Emma had to keep reminding herself not to ask about Braedon.

"Well," Kathy said as Emma was next in line to order, "we'll let you get back to your lunch."

Nodding, Emma gave them each another hug.

Before walking away, Jason turned to her and said, "He misses you like hell."

The words wiped the smile off of Emma's face. She swallowed hard to keep from crying.

"He looks the same way," he said sadly and turned to continue walking with Kathy.

Suddenly, Emma's appetite left her.

The clerk asked, "Ma'am, would you like to order?"

Emma just shook her head no and walked away.

Hours later, Emma finally parked in her garage and breathed a sigh of relief.

After her impromptu meeting with Jason and Kathy, she walked around the mall aimlessly for a good half hour before realizing she had to finish her shopping list.

To top it all off, she was scanning the list and came to Braedon's name since she made it out before their break up.

As soon as she came inside the house, she picked up the phone and called her dad.

He answered, "Hello there, daughter," on the third ring and she smiled.

"Hey, Dad," she said.

Tim knew when something was wrong with one of his daughters. He chalked it up to being a single parent for most of their teen years. He learned to read the signs in their voices.

He shut down the band saw he was using for a project that was to be a Christmas present for his middle daughter, Patty.

He stepped over to the shop stool the girls painted for him one year that said #1 Dad and asked Emma, "What's wrong?"

"How did you let her back in?" she asked.

Tim knew she was talking about her mother and he answered, "Because I love her."

Frustrated with his answer, Emma growled, "You have always said that!"

Smiling, Tim answered, "Because it was always true."

He heard his daughter sigh and knew he wasn't saying what she wanted to hear. People rarely did in his experience. That didn't mean you weren't honest but he'd always been honest with his girls.

"Listen," he said, "love is the hardest thing and the most rewarding thing. It makes you feel better than any drug on the market and it hurts like hell when it breaks."

"I know," Emma said.

She wasn't hearing him so he cooled his tone, "Emma listen to me," he waited for silence before continuing, "Your mom was mad because she couldn't control your future. It's not that she wished you to fail, she was just being stubborn when you didn't agree with her."

The tears she'd been fighting started to fall as Emma listened to her dad.

"I'll admit," he started, "taking this long to mend fences was a little drastic but neither of us could move on without the other one."

Emma nodded and sniffled.

Smiling, Tim said, "She realized that it wasn't about control, Emma, it was about acceptance. Letting someone love you is giving them full access to all of you, including your weaknesses. None of us wants to seem weak or let someone have that power over us but, sometimes, you just can't help it."

Listening to her dad, Emma wanted to say she understood, but she wasn't sure.

"After she left," Tim revealed, "I dove into work and taking care of you girls.....anything to make me not think about her." He waited a second before asking, "Does that remind you of anyone?"

Not wanting to admit she was wrong, Emma only mumbled, "Maybe," into the phone.

Her father laughed and said, "Emma, you got your mother's stubbornness and my innate ability to deflect energy into anything but what it should be put into."

She was getting the point but she didn't like it one bit.

There was one thing she was curious about so she asked her dad, "Are you happy, Dad?"

Just then his wife walked into the garage with a cup of coffee and a smile. It took less than a second for Tim to answer his daughter with, "Oh yes."

Chapter 31

Emma packed up her bag for the trip to New York and sighed.

She was in charge of getting the dresses there without incident and it scared the hell out of her. She even decided against a carry-on bag, instead she decided to take the garment bag with the dresses and keep it with her the whole way.

The wedding was on New Year's Day and Emma couldn't figure out why. There were like a gazillion people in New York for New Year's Eve and, to Emma's reasoning, a lot of them would still be there on New Year's Day. It was going to be a zoo.

She was flying in on the 29th so they could have the bachelorette party before New Year's Eve. With Eryn and Katherine getting bigger by the second, Emma wasn't sure how much "celebrating" they would do but it didn't matter anyway. Going out and partying wasn't big on Emma's to do list these days.

After arriving at the airport, Emma checked in without a problem. She was pretty sure she would've punched anyone who said anything about the garment bag but no one did.

She sat in the gate area and waited to board.

In New York, Beverly Fredricks knocked on the door of her daughter's hotel room.

She and her husband, Tom, flew in earlier that day. Beverly told Tom that she was going to help with the preparations. What he didn't know wouldn't hurt him in Beverly's eyes.

"Mom," Eryn said, surprised. She didn't expect her parents until the following day.

Entering the room, Beverly held her hands together in nervousness, "I think we need to go for a ride," she said to Eryn.

Eryn closed her eyes and sighed. Her mother tended to be an "arranger" and Beverly had that look on her face.

Grabbing her coat, Eryn kissed her husband goodbye and said, "Lead the way," to her mother.

Outside the hotel, Beverly asked the doorman to hail a cab for them.

"Are you going to explain?" Eryn asked her mother.

Smiling weakly, Beverly said, "You'll see."

Eryn had no doubt about that.

Thirty minutes later they stopped in front of a beautiful house on the Upper East Side.

Eryn looked at her mother with questions in her eyes.

Beverly just got out of the cab, paid the driver, and helped her daughter up the stairs to a lovely home.

After she knocked on the door, Beverly held her daughter close to keep the howling December wind from cutting through them.

The door opened and a lovely woman dressed in a uniform smiled, "Hello," she said, "you must be the Matron of Honor and her mother, Mrs. Fredricks."

Smiling, Beverly nodded and said, "We are, thank you."

Eryn thought maybe she stepped into the Twilight Zone. She had no idea where they were and what all the secrecy was about.

"I'm Helen," the woman said, "I'll show you to the parlor and let Master Gavriil and Miss Abigale know you're here."

Rolling her eyes, Eryn asked her mother, "Why didn't you just tell me we were going to Gav's parents' home?"

Beverly shrugged.

A few minutes later Abi and Gav came into the room and hugged Eryn and Beverly.

"Thank you," Gav said.

Beverly nodded and answered, "It's not a problem whatsoever."

"Okay," Eryn said suspiciously, "what's going on?"

Abi looked at her fiancé and Eryn's mother with pursed lips before saying, "I'll let the conspirators explain it to you."

Her brow creased, Eryn asked her mother, "What did you do?"

Smiling benignly, Beverly answered, "Just helped Gav with some arrangements."

Sighing, Eryn walked over and dropped into the closest chair. She took a deep breath and asked, "Okay, what's up?"

Abi grabbed the seating chart and brought it over to where Eryn was sitting. She didn't speak, just pointed to a spot on it and waited.

It didn't take long for Eryn to see what Abi was talking about. Her eyes shot up and pinned both Gav and her mother with her stare.

"What did you two do?" Emma asked. She looked over at Abi and sighed before she started to pray that this all worked out.

Abi grimaced and said to Gav, "You might as well tell her the rest."

Emma arrived at the hotel right on time. She had about two hours until she met up with the girls for dinner so she dropped her bags near the closet and went into the bathroom to shower and get ready.

She forgot to get her toiletry bag from her suitcase so she came back out, wrapped in a towel, and grabbed it before going back into the bathroom.

Braedon's plane landed a little early so he was glad to arrive at the hotel a little ahead of schedule. He was supposed to meet with the guys for dinner and drinks in a suite Gav reserved at the hotel.

He waited for Jason and Kathy to depart from the cab so they could all walk into the hotel together.

Kathy sighed when she met up with him before going inside. "This is gorgeous," she said.

Braedon nodded. This was all first class. Abi and Gav's parents were doing this wedding by-the-book. All of the wedding party's plane tickets and hotel rooms were paid for by the parents.

When Jason and Kathy received an invitation too, Abi's parents arranged for all three of them to travel together. He had spent a lot of time on the phone debating it with Gav but finally gave in.

Personally, he was relieved that he wouldn't have to endure this alone. Knowing Emma was going to be here was hard enough and having Jason and Kathy here kind of gave him "back up."

A concierge came over and introduced himself saying that he was personally in charge of guest lodging for the Maslov-Rochelle wedding.

They obediently followed him to the desk where they were issued keys. Jason tried to give his credit card for his room but the concierge refused and only said, "It's taken care of, sir."

The three of them looked at one another until they got into the elevator. When the doors closed, they broke out into laughter.

Although they were on the same floor, Jason and Kathy had a different room key.

The three of them waved goodbye and opened the doors to their rooms.

The first thing Braedon noticed was the shower was running. 'Great,' he thought, 'they gave me the wrong key.'

He walked over to the phone and pressed the extension the concierge gave him.

"Hello," he said when the line connected.

The concierge said, "Yes, Mr. Richards, how may I assist you?"

'Scary!' Braedon thought at first but he refocused and asked, "Uh, there's already someone in my room. Did you give me the right key?"

Knowing that he did not make mistakes, the concierge said, "Sir, some of the wedding party were scheduled to share rooms."

It sounded reasonable to Braedon so he just said, "Okay," and hung up the phone.

He decided, after tossing his bag in the closet so it didn't get mixed up with the other guy's stuff, to do a little sightseeing. He could get to know his roommate later.

Emma was just shutting off the water when she thought she heard the door to her room close. She hurriedly grabbed a towel and wrapped herself in it.

Slowly, she opened the bathroom door and peeked into the room. Thankfully it was empty and she sighed.

"Maybe it was the room next door," she said aloud and went back into the bathroom to finish getting ready.

She ended up going downstairs a few minutes early and, finally feeling more festive, she went into the bar off the lobby to have a cocktail. They were supposed to meet there anyway so one little drink wouldn't hurt.

Braedon walked into the lobby and almost ran smack dab into Abi. He smiled until he saw the look on her face.

"Braedon," Abi said while looking around the lobby.

"Uh yes," he said and leaned in to kiss her cheek.

As if she snapped out of her thoughts, Abi smiled and focused on him enough to say, "The guys are meeting upstairs in Gav's suite. Just go on up."

Clearly she was busy, so Braedon shrugged and went toward the elevators.

Eryn came up to Abi as Braedon got into the elevator and looked around, worried.

"No collision as of yet," Abi said and smiled weakly at her friend.

Nodding, Eryn clenched her hands together tightly in nervousness. She said, "You know, this could all blow up and she'll hate all of us."

Even knowing it was a long shot, Abi was willing to play along in the small hope that Emma might find happiness.

The friends walked into the club and found Emma at the bar.

"Hey," Emma said loudly and held up her glass, "these are sooooo gooood."

Eryn spoke first, "And it sounds like you've had a few of them."

Emma nodded. "I have indeed," she said and nodded to Eryn, "but unfortunately you can't have any."

Eryn sat on the stool beside her and sighed before saying, "Well then I guess you'll just have to drink my share."

Abi nodded to the bartender to make her one too and looked at Eryn. The silent look they gave one another was a mixture of relief and dread.

Katherine arrived along with a couple of Abi's friends who were guests for the wedding.

The women had a reserved table and sat down to wait for the live music to start.

Braedon knocked on the door to Gav's suite and smiled when Mitch opened the door.

"Hey, bud!" Mitch shouted and raised a bottle of beer.

Laughing, Braedon went inside and said, "I guess you started without me."

Mitch handed him a glass of beer and announced, "Hey everybody, Braedon's here."

There was a resounding "Hey!" from the crowd.

Braedon met a few of Gav's friends and watched Mitch to make sure he didn't get too drunk. A few minutes later, Gav and Chase came in.

"Braedon," Gav said and clapped him on the back and shook his hand.

Chase said hello and grabbed a beer while Gav poured himself a glass of Vodka. He laughed when Braedon's eyebrows rose and stated, "It's a Russian thing," before pouring glasses for all of them.

Hours later, none of them was making a whole lot of sense. Braedon really didn't care either. The numbness the alcohol caused was a welcome respite to the depression he had been feeling since he and Emma split.

He knew he would have to see her the next day for a dinner and that wasn't soon enough and all too soon at the same time. It was like he couldn't make up his mind where Emma was concerned.

Every time he mentioned her name, either Gav or Mitch or Chase poured him another drink.

After a while, he didn't care about anything except laughing.

Emma got back to her hotel room, but just barely. She never drank this much. Except that one time…..when she was with Braedon.

"No," she said out loud. Then smiled when a couple passed her and looked at her funny.

After a couple of attempts, she finally got the key card into the door and went inside.

The room was dark and she was glad. This would all be glaringly painful in the morning but, right now, it was so nice to not have to feel anything.

Stripping out of her dress, Emma pulled the pins out of her hair and dropped them on the floor as she made her way to the bed closest to the bathroom….just in case.

She managed to pull the sheets up around her before passing out.

"I gotta go," Braedon said to Gav.

Shaking his head slowly, Gav returned with a, "We just got started, buddy."

Laughing, Braedon said, "I'm done. Having a brother who owns a bar means that I figured out what my limit is a long time ago."

Mitch clapped a hand on his shoulder and said, "We get it, you have a good time."

Braedon looked at Mitch, confused.

Gav stepped forward and said, "He just means tomorrow."

Nodding, Braedon turned to leave the room.

Gav turned to Mitch and stared, "Dude, you almost ruined it!"

Shaking his head, Mitch said, "You're not supposed to mess with that stuff."

Gav snorted and asked him, "It got you and I a bride, didn't it?"

Reluctantly, Mitch nodded.

Braedon took the elevator down to the floor his room was on and hoped he would make it to bed without passing out. Here he was, talking to Gav about knowing your limits, and he pretty much exceeded his big time.

The elevator doors opened and he got out. He had to actually lean against the wall as he walked down to where his room was. He hoped his roommate didn't snore. It was probably one of the guys upstairs in the suite still partying.

Finally, he made it to the door and opened it quietly.

The lights were out and curtains drawn so it was pitch black inside his room. Before the door closed he thought he could make out a lump in the bed closest to the door.

He tried to walk quietly and slipped off his shoes near the door. He managed to get around the first bed and then he stepped on something.

"Ouch," he said loudly, then stopped to see if he woke up the guy sleeping.

Absently, he brushed off whatever was on the bottom of his foot.

When there was no other sound but breathing, he crept over to the other bed, stripped down to his underwear, and got in.

Thank goodness his roommate didn't snore.

Chapter 32

Emma woke up in increments. She got her eyes to open after rubbing the mascara off the lashes so they wouldn't stick together. The room was dark so she walked over to the window and opened the curtains.

Bright light poured into the room and she stared out the window. The busy street below mesmerized her with the movements of the people and vehicles.

She jumped when she heard a voice behind her say, "Good morning."

Yelping, Emma turned around, ready to defend herself when she saw the person was Braedon.

"What are you doing here?" Emma demanded.

Sitting up in the bed, Braedon stared at her. She looked crazy. Her hair was a nest of tangles, her eyes were smeared like a raccoon, and she probably felt as hung over as he did at the moment.

Of course, that didn't stop his traitorous body from responding to her the moment he laid eyes on her.

He slowly moved and said, "I could ask you the same thing."

Emma put her hands on her hips, clearly pissed, and said, "This is my room, Braedon!"

If she wanted a fight, then Braedon could oblige. He stood up slowly and mimicked her pose before saying, "It's my room, Emma!"

She wanted to be mad, she really did. But it was so difficult when they were both standing there, in their underwear, and hung over. Not being able to help it, she started giggling.

The minute Emma's face turned from rage to humor, Braedon knew he loved her. Loved her more than anyone else in the world, more than himself.

"I'm glad you're here," Braedon said slowly.

Emma just wondered how her life could possibly be this comical.

She suddenly felt self-conscious, but said, "I'm glad too."

He wanted to pull her to him but he was afraid she would reject him so he just stood there.

Inside, Emma knew she would have to be the one to make the moves. She was the one who ended it. But it was too scary, she didn't want to hurt anymore.

Still smiling, she excused herself and went into the bathroom.

Braedon watched her go into the other room and his hopes started to fall.

While she showered, Emma realized that her friends would need to be punished.....severely. The two pregnant ones would be spared for the moment but the bride-to-be was in a heap of trouble.

After she stepped out of the bathroom, Braedon went in and started the shower for himself.

Emma dressed in record time and pulled her hair back into a twist so she wouldn't have to fuss with it too much. She didn't know why the pins were on the floor but she picked them up and tucked them in a little bag she used.

When she was dressed and ready, she knocked on the bathroom door and said, "I'm meeting the girls so I'm going."

She heard Braedon say, "Okay," so she left the room.

Braedon came out of the bathroom once she left. He could still smell her perfume as it drifted around him. The sensation was pleasant and torture at the same time.

"Okay, Emma," he mumbled to himself, "what are we going to do now?"

Emma stepped of the elevator and into the lobby. She spotted a group of women at the far side and recognized Eryn's mother, Mrs. Fredricks, so she walked over to where they were gathered.

"Emma," Beverly Fredricks said before hugging Eryn's friend.

Smiling, Emma asked, "How are you today?"

Waving her hands, Beverly just smiled.

Beverly asked, "How are you today, dear?"

Shrugging, Emma answered, "We'll have to see."

'Cryptic,' Beverly thought.

Eryn and Katherine came over to the group and Eryn hugged her mother before looking at Emma.

Emma's gaze was stern and Eryn knew that Emma and Braedon had figured out they were in the same room.

Not saying anything, Eryn walked over to Abi's mother and greeted her.

"Chicken," Emma mumbled and pasted her best smile on.

Abi came in the front door to meet the group and made eye contact with Emma first thing. Busted!

Without saying anything, Abi pointed to Mrs. Fredricks.

Emma's eyes widened, confused.

Abi announced, "If you ladies will indulge me for just a few minutes, I'd like to have a word with my bridesmaids."

Everyone nodded and Abi corralled Eryn, Katherine, Emma, and Eryn's mother.

"I don't need to be here," Beverly said in an innocent tone.

Eryn pinned her mother with a stare and said, "This is your doing, you own up to it."

Once the five of them were away from the crowd, Emma started in with, "What the hell do you think you were doing?"

Abi hurt for her friend, it was plain to see that Emma was fighting back tears.

She asked Emma, "Did you two fight?"

Emma shook her head no, "Actually," she started, "we kind of laughed about it," she added when they smiled, "BUT, it's clear we both were upset with being duped!"

Eryn spoke up first, "Well, it was handled well enough. My mother pulled strings to make sure that Chase and I were stationed together."

Beverly started to shake her head no but stopped at the look her daughter gave her.

Katherine joined in with, "Mitch's mother asked me to see his family and made sure we met up at their house and lied to me about him not being there."

Nodding, Abi added, "And my parents friggin "promised" me to some guy I met when I was like two years old and put us in each other's way again."

Emma looked at all three of the most important friends she had. All three of them found the loves of their lives but it wasn't on their own.

She thought about what her dad said about how he put his energy into anything but love when it hurt. He also said that love never left unless you let it.

Beverly could see how conflicted Emma was about the situation and hurt for her. She was Eryn's friend so she was, by association, a daughter to Beverly. When Gav called her to say he thought Emma and Braedon should be together, she offered her assistance. If this ended up hurting Emma, then Beverly swore she would never meddle again.

Eryn finally asked the big question, "Em, do you love him?"

That question was not easy for Emma to answer. She just shrugged.

Her three friends hugged her tight and the group went back to join the others for the women's brunch they had planned.

The rest of the morning, Emma sort of walked around in a fog of thought.

She thought about Braedon, and all the wonderful things he did. How he knew when she needed space. How he pushed back metaphorically when she pushed him. How just the thought of him could make her smile, her heart pound, her pulse race, her hands get clammy, and her brain go foggy.

There was no mistaking how he made her feel when he made love with her. She remembered how he made her feel beautiful, not just on the outside, but on the inside.

Here was a man that volunteered to help others, worked hard, and loved his family.

Emma wanted to cry by the time the group left the restaurant. The others sort of let her be, she knew they were giving her space and she needed it.

Once they were outside, Emma picked up her phone and dialed.

The other line picked up with a bright, "Hello."

"Mom," Emma said, tears running down her cheeks, "I need your help."

Braedon met up with the guys at a pub a few blocks away from the hotel. Jason was supposed to go but he decided that he wanted to do some sightseeing with Kathy. Braedon was happy that the two of them were finally together but it left him out in the cold, so to speak.

He entered the building and was thankful for the heat. December in New York was a far cry from December in Southern California.

Seeing Chase, Braedon made his way over.

Once Chase saw him he asked, "Are you pissed?"

"Does everyone know?" Braedon countered.

Mitch and Gav walked over smiling but stopped when they saw Braedon's face.

Both Mitch and Chase pointed to Gav and said, "It was his idea," in unison.

Even though he wanted to be mad, Braedon couldn't be. These guys were good people who knew he loved Emma. He couldn't fault them for trying to help.

"Dammit," Braedon said loudly, "I love her!"

Patting Braedon on the back, Chase guided him over to a table.

They all sat down and ordered beers before Chase said, "You have now joined the club."

Gav and Mitch raised their glasses in salute.

If he didn't like them so much, Braedon was pretty sure he'd punch them.

"What the hell do I do about it?" he asked the three of them.

Leaning forward, Gav placed a piece of paper on the table and pushed it toward Braedon.

He looked at Mitch and Chase, who nodded, then said, "This is the number you call."

When Braedon picked up the paper, he almost choked on his beer. He looked up to see the three of his newest friends all nodding.

After the brunch excursion, the ladies in the wedding party all went back to the hotel and up to Eryn and Chase's room.

Emma darted back to her room to grab the bridesmaids' dresses and brought them up to Eryn's room where everyone was already gathered.

Handing the garment bag to Abi's mother, Emma joined Katherine and Emma in the other room to see Abi in her wedding gown.

"I hope you like it," Katherine said, her eyes dampening with tears.

Abi hugged her tightly and said, "I know I'll love it."

Emma yelled, "Let's see, let's see!"

Katherine walked around a room divider with Abi and her mother.

Emma and Eryn sat in chairs and were as fidgety as little kids.

Leaning over, Emma whispered to Eryn, "Wait until you see the bridesmaid's dresses."

They were chatting a few minutes later when Abi came out from behind the dressing screen.

There were no sufficient words to describe how Abi looked in the dress Katherine designed for her.

Emma gasped in awe. If she thought the bridesmaid dress was stunning, the only thing she could say about the bridal dress was, it was breathtaking.

"Oh, Abi," Eryn said while dabbing her eyes with a tissue.

The dress was done in ivory silk but had a gold brocade lace design on it. The top portion was fitted with an empire waist designed with a belt of gold and beads. There was a darker colored lace trip on the bottom or the flared skirt and that was matched by the lace on the cathedral length veil.

She looked like she stepped out of the nineteenth century, but still modern in the design.

"It's amazing," Abi whispered and spun around slowly.

Katherine fussed with possible details while they all stood and chatted around the bride.

Once Katherine was satisfied with the fit, Abi took her dress off and waited for the bridesmaids to preview their dresses.

The three of them stood behind the dressing screen and laughed as Eryn and Katherine tried to get their dresses on while accommodating their expanding waist lines.

Emma zipped up their dresses while Katherine zipped up Emma's.

They each did a turn in front of the bride and the mothers, who gushed over the dresses.

"I didn't think about the chest as much as the waistlines," Katherine said while trying to pull the fabric up over her now voluptuous chest.

Emma commented, "You got it for a change, flaunt it," and everyone booed.

After the fittings, the ladies parted ways for a few hours of free time before meeting up for dinner at a swanky restaurant downtown.

Emma hugged her friends and went downstairs to her room. She was still feeling sluggish from her drinking binge the previous night, but her attitude was better.

She spoke to her mother for a while as the women walked back from brunch and the conversation, although strained at points, was candid.

Emma appreciated her mother's openness in answering painful questions.

Things weren't completely settled between them, but the process of healing was definitely underway.

The conversation did something else too. It got Emma thinking about possibilities for a change instead of obstacles.

Chapter 33

Braedon got back to the room after lunch and was feeling a little better. Little being the operative word. Although hanging out with the guys was fun, they didn't do a whole lot to solve his current predicament.

He opened the door and stepped inside.

Emma was sitting in the chair across from the bed, thinking, when she heard the key card in the door. Nerves shot up her body and she was more scared than she could remember ever being.

When Braedon saw Emma sitting there, he stopped.

"Hi," Emma said and stood.

Snapping out of his love-induced trance, Braedon managed a returned, "Hi."

He looked serious, Emma noted. She probably looked the same.

Taking a step toward him, she said, "How was your lunch with the guys?"

Braedon watched her as she moved. She was graceful, like a ballet dancer, and he wondered if he ever told her that.

"It was fine," he answered, and asked her, "How was your brunch with the ladies?"

She took another step toward him and responded, "It was very nice; we tried on dresses."

Nodding, Braedon took a step toward her, "That sounds like fun," he said and added, "is the bride ready?"

"I think so," Emma answered.

Another step closer and she asked him, "How's the groom doing? Nervous?"

Braedon shook his head and stepped closer before answering, "He seems pretty steady."

They were about five feet apart now and stood there, standing at one another.

Finally, Emma said, "I spoke to my mother today."

Shocked by the admission, Braedon asked her, "How did that go?"

Emma shrugged but said, "It was difficult but I think we're on the road to forgiveness."

Relief poured into Braedon's chest. He worried about her making amends with her family. It was the situation he was thinking she may not make peace with and, the fact that she did, made him happy.

"Why are you smiling?" Emma asked him.

He looked at her, "Because you're happy," he answered in a low voice.

"I don't think so," Emma responded.

Braedon cocked his head, his brow crunched in confusion, and asked, "Why not?"

Emma closed the remaining space between them in a few steps. She was less than an arm's width away from him and she could hear his breathing and smell his cologne. All the parts of him that made him the best thing she'd ever come across in this lifetime.

"Because," Emma reached out and pulled his right hand up and held it between both of her palms, "you're not holding me and loving me."

Braedon's chest was tight with emotion but he managed to say, "I may not be holding you, Emma, but I'm always loving you."

Her chest heaved in a sob, "You are?" she asked.

Even though Emma was holding his hand in hers, he knelt down on one knee in front of her and said, "There is not one moment when my love doesn't surround you with all the love and comfort and support you need."

Tears ran down Emma's cheeks and she looked down into eyes that were as emotional as her own before asking, "Are you going to ask me to marry you or are you just practicing how to pray?"

Chuckling, Braedon shook his head. Was he ever going to be the one calling the shots? Probably not, but he would have fun trying.

"Emma Cantrell," he started, "I am down on my knee, my heart on my sleeve, your hand in mine, and with your daddy's blessing, to ask if you will marry me. I am willing to put up with your bullshit as long as you're willing to put up with mine."

Emma laughed. She was about as unconventional as could be so it should stand to reason that his proposal would be the same.

Nodding, Emma whispered, "Yes."

Braedon stood and took her into his arms and kissed her properly. His lips sealed his proposal. She was his and he was hers; Lord help them both.

Coming up from Braedon's kiss, Emma thought about what he said and asked, "What did you mean, my daddy's blessing?"

"I sort of called him earlier today and asked him if he would be okay with me marrying you," Braedon said as he laid his forehead against Emma's.

Chuckling again, Emma said, "I'll bet he was a little surprised."

He lifted his head and his hand to gently brush a tendril of her hair back away from her face.

"You know," Braedon said, recalling the conversation with Emma's father, "not really."

Emma laughed and brought his head down so she could kiss him again.

Their lips clung to one another as their hearts did, knowing that only they would be the one for each other, no matter what life threw at them.

An hour later, Emma and Braedon were running through the lobby of the hotel, on their way out.

Beverly Fredricks and her husband, Tom, were down there talking to friends when she saw the couple.

"I guess that means I don't have to stop," she said smugly.

Tom looked at his wife and asked, "I'm sorry, sweetie?"

Beverly looked at her husband, seeing only the beautiful man who decided to share his life with her years earlier and said, "Nothing, darling. Nothing."

Abi and Gav scheduled the rehearsal dinner for December 30th because New Year's Eve in New York City was just too crazy. They instructed their wedding party to live it up on New Year's Eve but everyone better show up at the designated time on the 1st for the wedding.

People were arriving for the dinner first and then everyone would go over to the church for the rehearsal.

Abi stood with her fiancé, so excited that day after tomorrow they would be married. The weather, although cold, did nothing to put a damper on her mood. The only thing she worried about was Emma.

Something happened after the brunch but Emma didn't talk to any of them about it. They made a pact to leave her alone about Braedon unless things got really stressed.

"Hey," Eryn said to Abi as she and Chase entered the private dining room for the dinner.

Abi smiled and said, "Hey yourself."

Nodding, Eryn spoke up, "I know, I was thinking about it all afternoon. Chase said no one has seen Braedon since lunch either."

Katherine and Mitch walked in and joined the group. She saw her friends and sighed.

"Are we thinking about Emma and Braedon?" Katherine asked.

With their heads nodding yes, Eryn and Abi followed the guys to the table. Everyone joined Gav's parents, who were already seated, and talking to Abi's parents. Eryn's parents were joining them as well.

The serving staff came around and took the orders for drinks.

A few minutes later, a winded Emma and Braedon blew into the room.

"I'm sorry," Emma announced, then added, "We were sightseeing and got distracted."

Eryn looked at Abi with a shocked look, then turned to look at Katherine and caught her surprised expression.

"That's quite alright," Isaak Maslov said as he stood and made a toast, "I'd like to drink to my son and his bride. May their home be blessed with joy and many grandchildren for his mother and I."

Everyone laughed.

Emma sat down next to Eryn and tried not to look at her friend.

Eryn waited for the group to take a sip before whispering to Emma, "Are you okay?"

Still trying to avoid looking Eryn in the eye, Emma nodded and took a sip from her water glass.

Abi's father stood then and made his toast. It was tearful and Abi cried as she got up to kiss her father on the cheek.

The announcement was made that everyone was requested to meet at the bride's family's house tomorrow morning for a Russian tradition.

Rolling her eyes, Abi just sighed. She understood her parents would want to honor some traditions from their homeland but her friends would probably think they were crazy.

A few minutes later, dinner was served.

Braedon sat across from Emma and couldn't stop smiling. He also couldn't stop staring at her. The afternoon was amazing but they decided not to share their engagement until after the wedding. Neither he nor Emma wanted to steal Abi and Gav's thunder.

They ate, sneaking glances at one another every few minutes.

Noticing, Mitch nudged Braedon and said, "Get a room."

Chuckling, Braedon replied, "We already have one."

Mitch laughed and turned back to his wife.

The rest of the dinner was uneventful. Everyone ate, then gathered to get their coats to go over to the church.

Since the restaurant was only two blocks from the church, they decided to walk. When the men made a stink about the pregnant women, both Eryn and Katherine blew them off, saying that walking was good for them.

Entering the church, Emma's eyes widened. It was huge!

There were at least thirty rows of pews on either side of the aisle. There were stained glass windows that flanked either side of the sanctuary that were at least twenty feet long. It was amazing and Emma knew immediately why Abi and Gav chose such a stunning venue for their wedding.

The priest was at the front of the church and greeted the group as they filed into the front pews. He went over the ceremony schedule and answered any questions.

Emma didn't realize that there was a traditional Russian custom that Abi and Gav wanted to integrate into their modern ceremony.

It was called The Crowning and it consisted of the matron of honor and best man holding crowns over the heads of the bride and groom. Then, the couple had to make circles to represent their entering into their married life.

After the explanation, everyone stood and lined up for the rehearsal.

Emma stood just behind Katherine and in front of Eryn in the processional line.

Not being able to resist being between the two very pregnant woman she turned to Abi and said, "This isn't contagious, is it?"

Abi laughed and was shushed by her father. He took his role seriously and wanted his daughter to do the same.

Emma made a face of mock terror and turned around to do her job as bridesmaid.

The pianist played the music and the women started moving down the aisle.

With the mostly empty church, the music reverberated off the walls and sounded magical.

Once everyone was lined up, the priest went over the specifics of the ceremony with Abi and Gav.

Emma stood in her place and stared at Braedon through the whole thing. She smiled dreamily at him as he spoke the vows for her friends, imagining she was saying them to Braedon.

Once the rehearsal was done, everyone gathered toward the back of the church, preparing to leave. Emma was talking to Katherine about the dresses when she noticed that Braedon wasn't with the group.

Looking around, she saw him standing at the front of the church, talking to both Eryn's mom, Mrs. Fredricks, and the priest.

For some reason, Emma suspected a plan was being hatched. Her eyes were intense as Braedon and Beverly made their way back to the group.

"What's going on?" Emma asked, her tone wary.

Beverly Fredricks waved her hand as if to dismiss their conversation with the priest and answered, "We were discussing music choices with the priest."

There was not one molecule in Emma's body that actually believed Eryn's mother. However, as long as the bride and groom were happy, Emma didn't care what plan she was hatching.

Braedon put his arm around her and guided her outside. The group was dividing up, the parents were going back to their respective homes, and the wedding party was going back to the hotel.

Emma waited until they were tucked into a cab before pinning Braedon with the question, "Fess up, what were the two of you plotting?"

Braedon tried to look innocent and said, "We were talking about marriages, Emma." Then he asked her, "Did you know that it only takes a day to get a marriage license to get married in the state of New York?"

Emma shrugged and answered, "Okay."

"You don't, by chance," Braedon asked, "have your birth certificate with you?"

Emma shook her head and answered, "No."

Braedon's face fell and he said, "Okay."

Wondering what he was talking about, Emma said, "It's not a big deal. I happened to be born here so I'm sure I can get a copy from the Department of Records."

Looking at Emma he asked, "I thought you were from Indiana?"

"I grew up there but I happened to be born here. Why?" Emma asked and thought maybe he had too much to drink.

He leaned over and kissed Emma deeply before saying, "You have no idea how happy you've made me."

The picture became clear and Emma looked at him with a shocked expression.

"Really?" she asked as the cab pulled up in front of the hotel.

Chapter 34

The morning of the 30th, the wedding party was busy. The men and women separated once again. The women went to Abi's parents' house for breakfast and to prepare for the Russian ceremony.

The men were eating at the hotel and meeting them there later.

Braedon walked in to see a clearly nervous looking Gav sitting at the table.

"Are you okay, man?" Braedon asked him.

Nodding, Gav answered, "Yes."

Not believing him, Braedon sat down beside him and offered a glass of ice water.

Gav sipped in and smiled in thanks before saying, "We're doing a ceremony this morning at Abi's parents' place and I'm worried."

Getting worried himself, Braedon asked, "What's going to happen?"

Mitch and Chase met up with them and sat down as Gav started to explain.

"It's called Paying the Ransom," Gav said and the three other men looked surprised.

He sighed, "Basically, I offer her father gifts for her hand in marriage," he said in a rushed voice.

"That doesn't sound too bad," Braedon said.

Tilting his head back and forth, "It's not really," Gav said, "It's more like, I need to make sure what I offer is good enough for Mr. Rochelle."

Mitch let out a whistle and added, "I'm glad I didn't have to do that with Katherine's parents. I'm pretty sure her father would have said no to anything fewer than two million."

The men laughed and Gav seemed to settle down after that.

They ate and got into a cab to go to the "Ransom Ceremony."

After arriving at the building where Abi's parents lived, the men were buzzed in by the doorman. They got into the elevator with Chase, Mitch, and Braedon cracking jokes to keep Gav's nerves in check.

Gav knocked on the door and the group were greeted by Abi's father. He made a production out of escorting the men into the living room.

The ladies were all seated and watched Gav as he walked over to kiss, first his parents, then Abi's mother in greeting.

Clearing his throat, Gav said, "Sir, I'm here to pay the ransom for Abi's hand."

Standing tall, Andrei Rochelle asked, "What have you brought?"

Gav's father stood up and stepped over so he was next to Gav. He had two small boxes with him and handed one to Gav.

"I present this gift to Abigale," Gav said in a somewhat shaky voice.

He opened the box and showed everyone.

Emma's eyes widened when she saw the contents. It was a gorgeous diamond bracelet.

Andrei nodded and motioned for Abi to come out.

She came out and was completely covered in white from head to toe. The veil was so thick, you couldn't even see her face.

Presenting Abi to Gav, Andrei nodded and allowed Gav to lift the veil.

Everyone laughed when it was a friend of Abi's under the veil, who also happened to be a guy, who puckered up for Gav's kiss.

Rolling his eyes, Gav said to his father, "Ah, now I know why there are two boxes."

Isaak beamed and gave his son the other box.

Gav opened up this box and everyone did oohed and ahhed. Inside, was a beautifully intricate diamond necklace that matched the bracelet.

Andrei, once again, nodded and then Abi did come out of the other room and was presented to Gav. She started to cry when she saw the jewelry and hugged Gav and his parents.

"I guess it helps if your dad owns a diamond business," Emma whispered to Eryn, who nodded in response.

After the ceremony was over, everyone was offered food and drink.

Braedon walked over to where Emma was talking to Abi's mother and gently took her elbow.

Excusing herself, Emma asked Braedon, "What's up?"

Looking around to make sure they weren't overheard, Braedon whispered, "I'd like you to take a trip with me."

Smiling, Emma assumed he was speaking about some alone time back at the hotel. They didn't get much sleep the night before because of meeting up with Jason and Kathy for drinks then taking a long stretch of "alone time."

Who was she to refuse? "Okay," she answered him.

They walked out of the apartment after making their excuses. When they got downstairs, Jason and Kathy were waiting with a cab.

Emma looked at them, then at Braedon, her eyes questioning.

"You trust me, right?" he asked her as he opened the door of the cab.

Smiling, Emma answered, "Implicitly," and got in.

Hours later, Emma, Braedon, Kathy, and Jason arrived back at the hotel. The afternoon was productive and Emma couldn't believe how much Braedon took care of.

Were they really going to get married here in New York before going back to California? Emma still couldn't believe it.

They walked into the club off the lobby and saw Eryn, Chase, Abi, Gav, Mitch, Katherine, Mr. and Mrs. Fredricks, and Mr. and Mrs. Maslov sitting at a table.

Everyone stood when the foursome walked over and started clapping.

Emma looked at her friends, then at Braedon. She should have known they couldn't get anything over on them.

"Funny," Emma said dryly.

"We thought so!" Eryn shouted in return.

Braedon left Emma's side and walked over to where Mr. Maslov was standing. Emma saw Gav's father hand Braedon a box and she couldn't help but start to cry.

He walked over and, in front of everyone, opened the box to show a beautiful set of rings.

They were the most perfect rings Emma could ever imagine. The bridal set was done in white gold with a large diamond in the center and a band with small diamonds to match. The ring that Braedon would wear was a perfect match.

"Oh," Emma said as Braedon pulled out the engagement ring and slid it onto her finger.

Abi started sniffling and nudged Gav for a tissue.

Emma thought everyone would sit down after the ring thing but they all stood there as if they were waiting for something.

Looking around, Emma finally asked, "What?"

Beverly Fredricks spoke up first and said, "You know, there are some people who are doers and some people who are planners."

Emma watched Eryn's mother curiously.

"You realize, Emma, that you are standing in a room with both of those kinds of people?" Beverly said with a smile.

Emma nodded but was still confused.

Eryn stepped over to her friend and said, "What my mother is trying to say in her dramatic way is that you have a personal jeweler," she pointed to Mr. Maslov, "your personal dress designer," she pointed to a beaming Katherine, "and a group of people who have nothing better to do than ensure you actually walk down the aisle to marry this man," she pointed to Braedon, "who's crazy enough to want to stick with you for the rest of your life."

Looking at Braedon, Emma's tears were the happiest ones she ever shed. She looked at every person here and they were all willing to do anything for her. How did she get so lucky?

Snapping out of her emotional cloud, Emma said, "Okay, then, let's do this!"

The crowd clapped and crowded around them.

At 11:55pm on New Year's Eve, Braedon and Emma stood at the altar of the Church.

Emma wore a beautiful dress Katherine had sent over from her design studio in New York. It was pure white, with flowers of beads and crystals down the front. They paired it with a faux mink wrap.

She also found dresses for Abi, Eryn, herself, and Kathy to wear for the occasion.

Beverly Fredricks went to school with a judge in New York who was willing to push through their marriage license and took care of securing the church.

Mrs. Maslov knew the owner of a local flower shop and made sure there were bouquets.

The priest was kind enough to arrange for a pianist to come in and play for the ceremony.

Before they started, Emma took Abi aside and asked, "Are you sure we're not stepping on your toes here?"

Abi hugged her friend, "Are you kidding me, I am winning a hundred dollar bet with Gav on whether you would go through with this."

They laughed but Emma looked at her, the question still in her eyes.

"You aren't stepping on anything," Abi said and held Emma's hands.

Eryn and Katherine flanked them on either side.

Abi looked at her friends, her sisters, and said, "This will be the best year ever, we're all going into it with the best kind of love there is.......true love."

"Amen to that," Eryn whispered to her friends.

Katherine added, "The baby is kicking so it must be good."

They laughed and turned to walk down the aisle to where Braedon, Jason, Chase, Gav, and Mitch stood smiling.

The ceremony was small and intimate. Braedon and Emma spoke their vows clearly.

Mr. and Mrs. Fredricks sat in the front pew of the groom's side and held up IPads. One was Skyping with Emma's family in Indiana and one was streaming to Braedon's family in West Virginia so everyone they loved could be there.

Braedon slipped the ring on Emma's finger just as the clock started ringing midnight.

The priest announced them husband and wife and told them they could kiss.

Braedon smiled at Emma and whispered, "Happy New Year, Wife."

Emma whispered back, "Happy New Year, Husband," before kissing him deeply.

Applause broke out and everyone congratulated the couple.

The group went back to the hotel, where a table was reserved for the celebration.

They danced and celebrated until after three in the morning when Abi and Gav told everyone they had to get up for another wedding in a few hours.

Braedon carried his bride across the lobby, ignoring the applause from the staff and other guests, and directly into the elevator. He held her in his arms during the ride up to their room and carried her down the hall.

"You know," he said as he fumbled with the key card while holding Emma in his arms, "they wanted to get us a suite but I told them no thanks."

Emma mocked a pout and asked, "Why?"

He opened the door and carried her inside. When he set her down, she looked around the room, her mouth dropping open. There were roses everywhere.

Braedon whispered in her ear, "Because I didn't want to move the damn flowers."

Looking at her husband, Emma thought he was brilliant and she proceeded to show him how much.

On January 1st, everyone met up to get ready for Abi and Gav's wedding.

Exactly at 1:00pm, Katherine began the processional at the church. She was followed by Emma, then Eryn. The bride practically floated down the aisle in her beautiful ivory and gold dress.

They were listening to the vows when Emma looked over to see her husband looking at her.

She mouthed, "I love you," to him then directed her attention back to the bride and groom.

After the first part of the ceremony, Eryn handed her bouquet to Katherine and handed Abi's to Emma before following Abi up the steps to the altar area.

They watched as crowns were held over Abi and Gav's heads and they were guided around the altar.

When the ceremony was done, and the priest announced them man and wife, Abi and Gav kissed.

The recessional music played and the wedding party started back down the aisle.

Emma met up with Braedon and they started the trek down the aisle before he leaned over to say, "You look very beautiful, Wife."

Looking at her husband, Emma replied, "You look pretty hot yourself, Husband."

They stopped so a picture could be taken by the photographer before starting again.

Emma looked at Braedon and asked, "Do you feel like we've been here before?"

He shook his head and wondered how he got so lucky to have such a smartass as a wife.

Dear Readers:

This series is very special to me. It really was the spark that started my dream of being a writer. I hope you've laughed and cried at the adventures of Eryn, Katherine, Abi, and Emma as much as I have. I cannot help but see how there is nothing in our life as wonderful as friendship.

This book was supposed to be the last one in the Semper Fi in Love series but I already have questions about what happens next. Perhaps we'll meet up with the characters again………

I wish all of you the best in your life and especially in your love.

Best Wishes,

Danette